BIBLICAL THEMES
... AND OTHERS

A BOOK OF POEMS

by

John Cowell

Best Wishes
John

RB
Rossendale Books

Books by John Cowell

The Broken Biscuit

Cracks In The Ceiling

Elephant Grass

An American Journey

My Camino Amigo

Clogs And Shawls

Ups And Downs Of A Poker Player

Emma

My Life In Verse

Poemsof Life

A Compilation of poems

Poetical themes

My entire Life in verse

Published by Amazon KDP Publishing
In association with Rossendale Books

Published in hardback 2024
Category: Poetry
Copyright John Cowell © 2024
ISBN : 9798339282310

All rights reserved, Copyright under Berne Copyright Convention and Pan American Convention. No part of this book may be reproduced, stored in a retrieval system, or transmitted in any form or by any means, electronic, mechanical, photocopying, recording or otherwise, without prior permission of the author. The author's moral rights have been asserted.

TEMPTATION

Temptation is a desire to do something wrong or unwise and yet we are all prone to succumb to it.

A quote by Oscar Wild sums it up perfectly:

I can resist anything except temptation

To express what I think about poetry I say it to you in verse:

POETRY

Expressions come from within one's inner self
Pure thoughts cannot be bought with money,
Wisdom used in poetic verse
Is likened to nectar and honey.

Introduction

My name is John Cowell. I was born in Burnley, a Lancashire cotton town, on 11th April 1939 just before the outbreak of the Second World War. Times were hard but there was a good community spirit and people gathered together and helped each other out as best they could. My teenage years were great. I feel sorry for today's teenagers. In my young days we had picture houses, youth clubs and dance halls where we danced to the fantastic sound of big band music. What have the young ones got today? Very little, or so it seems, but then again I may be biased. I have had a varied life. I was born in a two up two down terraced house smack right in the middle of the 'Weaver's Triangle,' a busy cotton community. There were more tall factory chimneys in Burnley than any other town, of comparable size, in the world.

My family consisted of my parents, two brothers and three sisters. I spent nine years as a coalminer interrupted by two years National Service in the Royal Army Medical Corps and spent most of my army time in Cameroon, West Africa. I worked a few years as a self

employed joiner and then at the age of 38 I entered the nursing profession and worked on Accident and Emergency as a staff nurse. Upon my retirement I fulfilled a promise to my mother and wrote her biography .... 'The Broken Biscuit.'
I still live in Burnley.

Foreword

I have never classed myself as a writer and yet I have now written several stories and a few poems. My inspiration to write came from two ladies whom at different times of my life became my partner.

The first lady was Ann and she encouraged me to write 'The Broken Biscuit.' It is a biography of my mother's life. After it was published it surpassed all my expectations. Sadly though, I was with Ann for 15 years and she died a few weeks after my first book was published. I will be totally grateful to her for the remainder of my life.

Here is a verse that that I composed and read out at her funeral.

MY GENTLE ANN

Despite your illness ... your sorrow and pain
Not once to me did you e'er complain
Each day you greeted me like the morning dew
Never again will the sky appear quite so blue

Just as the planets revolve around the sun
We mingled ... we laughed ... we became as one
In my heart you'll remain with me till life's end
My love ... my life ... my true devoted friend

The second lady to inspire me is my wife Elsina. I had already written several books when I met her and I was totally committed to retiring. However, after reading my stories and poems she insisted that I write on.

And so be it, that's exactly what I did. I wrote many funny verses and poems about nature. But then from out of nowhere I got this inspiration to write biblical themes and once I'd started I could not put my pen down

To me, God is love and God is nature and that is why I enclose many poems relating to nature and how it affects all mankind.

I am now eighty-five years old and I feel this may be my last book. Therefore I sincerely hope you enjoy it and get some benefit from it.

May God bless you!

THE OLD TESTAMENT

GENESIS
In the beginning God created the heavens and earth
Just waste, void and darkness filled the abyss
God reached forth with all his worth
And gently touched the firmament with a gentle kiss
God said let there be light and so it was so
He saw it was good and called the light day
Light sparkled with an eminent special glow
Universe twinkled with a brilliant God given spray
God separated the dark from the vast empty waste
And he named the darkness night
He placed stars in the heavens sparkling and chaste
Light formed a day e'er so vibrant and bright
He then separated the firmament from the sea
And created the heavens in the sky above
Stars floated over e'er so bright and free
A universe fashioned by God's undying love
God then divided the oceans e'er so wide
And in between he made land arrive
Land and sea now a great open divide
God saw that his vision was e'er so wise

He viewed the barren land dead with needs
And wasn't pleased by what he saw
So he spoke and behold ... many life-giving seeds
Sprang to being with a life-giving glow
It was good to see vegetation and trees
Fruit and flora throughout the land
Beautiful vistas of mountains and vast open leas
Complimented by beaches of sparkling white sand
God in his infinite wisdom created beings by and by
"Let waters abound with life!" he stressed
"Let winged creatures be abundant in the sky
Let all land, sea and sky for e'er be blessed"
He spoke and many living creatures came forth
Wild animals, reptiles, snakes and cows
God saw it was good and knew in due course
'Twas time to make man ... 'twas one of his vows
He spoke again and man began his life
And God gave him dominion o'er every creature around
Yet man was lonely so God gave him a wife
And together they were steadfastly bound
God gave them leave to be fruitful in love
To fill the entire earth and sub due it
To live alongside creatures from above
And fashion the earth from dust and grit

He gave them both every seed-bearing shrub
And to every creature an abundance of fare
Adam and Eve became a world bearing hub
And God gave them control o'er earth's wear and tear
Earth and the heavens now were complete
God was happy with the work he had done
'Twas a tremendous effort ... a glorious treat
And He relaxed 'neath a sparkling white sun

ADAM & EVE

In the beginning God created the heavens and the earth
The earth was nought but darkness and abyss
The Lord blessed it with all his worth
And created light with a loving kiss
He then made land to divide the seas
After creating water 'neath a heavenly sky
Then He made dry land appear in a breeze
'Twas a haven for mankind so high and dry

God said, *Let the waters abound with life*
Let winged creatures fly around the firmament
Sea creatures of all kinds were healthy and rife
'Twas a paradise so heavenly sent
He created all creatures and wild beast
Even reptiles and snakes with a typical hood
An abundance of plants from the soil did yeast
And God looked around and saw it was good

Then God in His wisdom brought forth man
He breathed into his nostrils and gave him life
The man was lonely and in need of a clan
So God breathed again and made him a wife

God named the man Adam and called his wife Eve

For them he created many fruits to grow on the land
Life giving plants did flutter and weave
Food in abundance like tiny grains of sand,
God granted them dominion over all wildlife
Over every living creature in the sea
Custodians of all were Adam and his wife
Over every patch of land, meadow or lea

God planted a garden in Eden to the east
'Twas a paradise to Adam and his wife
All kinds of food to supply a ravenous feast
Amongst all these was the tree of life
But The lord commanded the pair thus
From all the shrubs in the garden you may eat
But this tree is bound and locked by a truss
To eat from it is a forbidden treat

Both the man and woman were naked bare
But in their innocence they felt no shame
Now the serpent was more cunning than any wild bear
And to tempt Eve was his direct aim

And he said to Eve in a devious way
Did God say thou must not eat from that tree?
Eve replied that to eat from it, with her life she wouldst pay

But the devil tempted her more so open and free
The serpent assured her she would not die
Thy eyes will be opened and thou shalt be like God himself
And thy knowledge will rise way up high
Thou shalt obtain magic and power like a fairy elf

To Eve the tree was pleasing to the eye
And she yearned for the knowledge it would accord
She took of the fruit and ate it nigh
And Adam did the same and offended The Lord
Both their eyes were opened and they realised they were bare
So they made coverings out of fig leaves
And both hid themselves from The Lord's glare
But God espied them and He was filled with grief

The Lord asked Adam, *Where are you?*
Adam replied that he was naked and bare
God asked him of his nakedness and how he knew
'Twas the serpent who deceived us and this I swear

Then God approached the serpent in the grass
And because of its evil he cursed it
On thy belly forever thou shalt crawl and pass
And hence shall be cast into a bottomless pit

Adam and Eve, the first two humans alive
He banned them from the heavenly paradise
From thence they had to toil and strive
'Twas the price they paid for their devious vice

Adam knew Eve and she bore him a son
And she called the man-child Cain
She prayed to The Lord under a setting sun
For helping her deliver through anguish and pain
Later she gave birth to Abel
And he hence became a keeper of sheep
Then something happened ... a terrible fable
An awful deed to make Adam and Eve lament and weep

Cain was jealous of Abel and in a terrible rage
He took up a weapon and slew his brother
'Twas the first murder in the biblical age
And it brought sadness and grief to father and mother

The Lord condemned Cain for his brother's blood
And he cast him out from the land he plod
From thence it was hard to create e'en a minute bud
And for life thereafter Cain dwelt in the land of Nod

Adam lived nine-hundred and thirty years old

NOAH

Noah was a good man in every way
He lived by the word of The Lord
Alas, all around sinned and cursed every day
They lived not by love but by the edge of the sword
When God saw that the evil in men was so great
He regretted He had created man's birth
Being grieved he determined another fate
To totally wipe out man from the earth

However, Noah found favour in his heart
As he was a just, blameless man
He was the father of three sons in part
Sem, Ham and Japheth were of his clan
The earth was corrupt and full of wrath
And God told Noah of his scheme
He informed him of a different path
An ark to be built by Noah and his team

Make an enormous ark of resin-wood
And cover it with pitch inside and out
Make it invulnerable 'gainst tempest and flood
Three-hundred cubit's long 'ere so firm and stout

The ark to be fifty cubit's wide
And thirty cubits shall it be high
Make an opening door to its side
Make sure 'tis strong, stable and dry
Also it shalt have sturdy floors three
A bottom, a second and a third level
Thou shalt work on it like a busy bumble bee
'Twill avail 'gainst constraints of the devil

For in truth I shall bring flood upon the earth
Under heaven I wilt destroy all mortal flesh
Departed will be souls to which I gave birth
And the world will have to be reborn afresh
I will make a covenant with you
Thou shalt enter the ark with your sons and wife
Of every living creature you shall bring two
And thou shalt care for them throughout heartache and strife

Take every kind of food with you and store it
Enough to serve both the animals and thy kin
Take heed and serve portions bit by bit
And lead a heavenly life free from evil and sin.

Seven days after entering the ark
The waters of the flood poured down upon the earth
The floodgates of heaven opened and hit their mark
And the waters abounded around the ark's girth
All the fountains of the great deep burst forth
Rain fell onto the earth for forty days and forty nights
And covered the earth south, west, east and north
Nowhere could be seen any beautiful sights

Noah was six-hundred years old
When the heavens opened and cloud-breaks burst
Enclosed now in the ark with his wife and fold
'Twould be forty days before the tempest weather reversed
The waters rose fifteen cubits above the mountains
All flesh that moved on the earth had died
No sign of life near to glorious fountains
For a while, Noah openly sighed and cried
After forty days Noah opened the door
And from thence he released a raven
He cast it out and away it did soar
But alas, it found no nestling place or haven

The waters covered the earth for 150 days
Then God remembered Noah and his kin

And he sent a strong wind with spiritual ways
And the waters resided in a miraculous spin
The waters continued to reside for seven months
And the ark rested on the top of Mount Ararat's peak
Noah did espy the earth on all fronts
And decided to view it within another week

He waited yet another seven days and seven nights
And beheld a dove within his vein
He sent it forth to discover any new sites
And this time she returned with a tiny olive grain
Seven days later he sent the dove out once more
But he'd set eyes on her for the last time
As she didn't return from her heavenly chore
And Noah knew he was in for an arduous climb

After two months Noah opened the door
And saw that all the ground's surface had dried
He and his family descended to the floor
And all together they prayed and openly cried

First thing he did was to set the animals free
He then built an altar to offer God his thanks
To live a life of integrity was his decree
To be honest and sturdy as solid river banks
Noah's sons and their wives didst populate the earth

And God fearing nations did unfold
Noah strived to lead a holy life
When he died he was nine hundred and fifty years old

ABRAHAM

After Cain murdered his brother Abel
God exiled him from The Promised Land
From thence his future lay in the land of Nod
A vast barren desert of fierce winds and gritty sand
About two thousand years later, God gave Abraham an order
Get thee out of thy country unto a land I will show thee
Abraham obeyed and sought out Chanaan's border
A sand laden place near to the Red Sea

After Abraham reached Chanaan, God made him a promise
Henceforth; Chanaan was called The Promised land
To later bring Israelites was a compromise
'Twas a master plan laid out by God's hand
Abraham had incredible faith and righteousness was imputed unto him
A divine sceptre was his guiding rod
A brilliant glow flowed fro' every limb
Henceforth he was called the friend of God

After victories over four powerful Assyrian kings
Abraham befriended Melchizedek, a most high priest
And both sang lyrics as a skylark sings
During festivities and a celebrity feast

Melchizedek was a high priest of celestial being
And a bond formed with Abraham so special indeed
Together they begat holy blessings spiritual
Their friendship highlighted a heavenly creed
Abraham and Melchizedek were special friends indeed
Their friendship was blessed from heaven above
'Twas sacred and evolved from an angelic seed
And their countenance was one of purity and love

In records discovered by Jews in the first century BC
Was a text written in the Dead Sea Scrolls
Many Jews likened it to a blessed family tree
Believing fervently as a church bell tolls
They believed Melchizedek was a spiritual being
In their minds he was the true Jesus Christ himself
His countenance was aluminous and all seeing
And depicted a scene of love, truth and health

Abraham loved family and yearned for a son
Yet for decades his wife Sarah could not bear a child

Abraham was one-hundred years old when Isaac was born
Underneath an array of stars in cosmos wild

It is easy for an old man to almost worship a son
Especially an Adonis, strong with purity of mind
Isaac was indeed a beam of light from the sun
To Abraham he was a star ... a very special kind
But then God put to Abraham a test to heed
A test unlike what he had given to any other soul
To sacrifice his only son in a faithful deed
In order to carry out The Lord's heavenly call

God said, *Take thy only son whom you love*
And go unto a place somewhere way up high
There offer him up to me like a turtle dove
Upon a mountain, Isaac wilt surely die
And they came to the place that God had bade
Abraham built an altar and laden it with wood
He then laid Isaac out and lifted his blade
In his mind Abraham had already shed Isaac's blood

Then an angel of The Lord called onto him from above
Abraham, lay not thine hand upon the lad
For now I knowest thou fearest The Lord with love

God breathed and Abraham became e'er so relieved and glad

This was an act of faith like none other
'Twas an example to bring faith alive
An act like a love 'tween sister and brother
An act to encourage faith to up and thrive
Despite Abraham's age, God made a promise to him
Your descendants will be as numerous as the stars
Through Isaac, Jacob and Joseph the promise was passed down
Descendants uncountable like dust particles on Mars

Abraham died at a good age of one-hundred and seventy five years
His kinsmen buried him in Ephron within a cave
After his death, God didst bless Isaac
And the man grew to be strong, faithful and brave

SODOM AND GOMORRAH

Sodom and Gomorrah were cities full of vice and sin
God looked down from heaven with a sigh
He decreed the destruction of every family and kin
Every soul within each city would perish and die
Abraham approached The lord and said
Will you destroy the just along with the evil and bad
If I can recall fifty just men to head
Would it stop Thee doing something so sad

Said The Lord *Far be it to treat wicked and just the same*
I wilt spare them for the sake of just fifty men
And wilt release them fro' a fiery flame
And allow them life in a beautiful green glen
And Abraham spoke to The Lord again
And if forty were to be found there
God replied like the stroke of a pen
For forty just men, their lives I will spare

Abraham paused and then spoke again
Please Lord do not be angry if I say
What if thirty cause no sorrow or pain
God replied *There be no harm to them this day*

Abraham asked again for just twenty or ten
And The Lord allowed it to be so
Nothing will happen for the sake of ten just men
And Gomorrah's lifetime wilt up and flow
But the evil in the city was e'er so great
Not even ten men couldst be found
Because the evil within was so full of hate
God decided to raze the city to the ground

Two angels appeared to Lot at night
He was sitting on a stool near to a gate
When he espied them it gave him such a terrible fright
That he bent to his knees and then fell prostrate
He baked unleavened bread and prepared a meal
Then some townsmen of Sodom came with hate in their soul
They were aggressive with eyes hardened like steel
To abuse the two men-angels was their goal

Please I beg thee, do not harm these men
They have come under the shelter of my roof
But the men were determined to enter Lot's den
And their vile anger displayed the living truth

They pressed hard against Lot as he stood by the door
But an angel drew him back into the home
And those on the outside were struck blind to the floor
From the least to the greatest, none could neither see nor roam
Both angels of The Lord appealed to Lot
And advised him to gather his family and flee
Sulphur and fire will rain down e'er so hot
And destroy the city and every dale and lea

One also advised Lot's two intended brothers-in-law
About the terrible thing they were about to ordain
But they thought he was jesting and refused to go
So they were about to perish along with the vain
The two angels took Lot's family by the hand
And led them beyond the city's border
One angel said, *Flee for thy lives or die in the sand*
For we are about to destroy the cities under God's order

Lot planned to head for Segor, a small place
And the angels urged him to move quickly on his way
They promised him safety with a warm embrace
And warned them not to look back or sway

Lot fled with family to a tiny city
Segor was the name of the place
He thanked The Lord for his guidance and pity
And they settled therein to live life with a warm embrace
Alas, on leaving the city condemned to die
They'd been advised not to look back or malt
Lot asked the angel the reason or why
Still, his wife looked back and turned into a pillar of salt

ISAAC

Abraham knew his wife Sara and she conceived
She bore a son in Abraham's old age
They blessed the boy with the name Isaac
And like his father he became a holy sage
Sara was overjoyed with the child's birth
As Abraham was one-hundred years old
She praised The Lord with all of her heart
The child to her was worth his weight in gold

The child grew and was lovingly weaned
Abraham threw a glorious feast that day
Henceforth the boy grew to be healthy and strong
And The Lord guided him in a heavenly way
Isaac was forty years old when he married Rebecca
He craved for a son but it appeared not to be
As Rebecca his wife could not bear a child
Their hopes seemed dashed in the deep blue sea

The Lord appeared to Rebecca and said
Two nations are within thy womb
Two sons shalt stem from thy body
Their lives wilt dispel all gloom and doom

One son shalt be stronger than the other
And the elder will serve the younger son

Rebecca told Isaac of her vision
And he rejoiced 'neath a setting sun
At the time of her delivery she did have twins
The first to come forth was stocky and red
His entire body was like a hairy garment
They named him Esau in his stead

The second came forth gripping Esau's heel
Both sons were honoured and lovingly adorned
Jacob was to be the younger brother's name
Isaac was sixty years old when they were born
When the boys grew up into manhood
Esau became a skilful hunter of game
Whilst Jacob was happy amongst the tents
Isaac loved Esau because of his wildness and fame

Rebecca noticed Isaac's attitude towards the lad
And she turned her affection to Jacob more
Esau loved to be with nature out in the wild
And of his birthright, Jacob did implore

One day whilst Jacob was cooking food
Esau came from the fields with hunger and thirst

He begged Jacob for something to eat
Jacob gave him a meal but requested something first
Jacob said, *Sell me first thy birthright*
Esau shrugged and replied, *What worth is it to me*
Jacob asked Esau to swear and he did so
Then he ate and felt happy and free

Jacob had only given him some bread and lentils
And Esau ate the food and gave up what was his due
Thus so lightly did Esau value his birth-right
He's sold it for a pot of stew
Time passed quickly and Isaac was old and frail
His eyesight had failed and he was blind
He asked Esau to come by his side
And said he wanted to make a heavenly bind
Said Isaac, *You see that I have grown old*
Take up thy weapons, quiver, bow and tie
Go out in the fields and hunt me some game
That I may bless thee before I die

But Rebecca was listening and after Esau left
She bade Jacob to do as she say
She then clothed him in Esau's garments
And put kid's skins on his hand that day
Jacob approached his father with savoury food

And Isaac was confused by Jacob's voice
But when he felt at his hairy hands
He felt sure he had made the right choice

When he smelt the fragrance of Esau's garments
The redolence of the fields overcame him
He kissed Jacob and gave him his blessing
Jacob had betrayed his brother with a sin
Spoke Isaac, *May God give thee dew from heaven*
And bless thee with fruitfulness of the earth
Let all nations bow down before thee
Be the master of all thy kin with all its worth

Isaac had just pronounced the blessing
When his son Esau entered the house
When he approached, Isaac asked, *Who art thou*
Esau answered, *I am the first born of thy spouse*

Then whom *have I just blessed, asked Isaac*
Esau exploded into a bitter cry
Father bless me too for I am thy first born
Give me thy blessing lest I should die
Father, Jacob has now supplanted me twice
And this time he taketh my rightful blessing from me
I know Jacob's blessing is fixed in law
But he was deceitful and stole it from thee

27

Hence, Esau bore Jacob a grudge
He hated Jacob for what he had done
And swore that after Isaac passed away
He wouldst surely kill Jacob by rule of thumb
Rebecca was aware of how Esau felt
And so she summoned her younger son
Your brother Esau seeks to kill thee, she said
Thou must pack up now and go on the run

So Jacob did as his mother said
And he fled to where his uncle did dwell
He waited until after his father had died
Who'd blessed him to avoid the fires of hell
Isaac was sad and he called for Jacob
And he forgave him before he died
He also told him to head for another land
Jacob took his advice and openly cried
Shortly after Isaac died and left this earth
And he was buried within his father's cave
He now lay beside his father, Abraham
Two sages together holy and brave

Isaac lived to be one-hundred and eighty years old

JACOB

After the death of Isaac, Jacob fled to Laban's place
He had sinned and ran off to escape Esau's hate
His elder brother whom he had offended
And stolen his blessing, birthright and fate
On his journey to a far distant land
He came across a nice shady place
The sun had set so he spent the night
And for a pillow he placed a stone 'neath his face

He dreamed of a ladder stood on the ground
With its top reaching way up to heaven above
Angels waltzed up and down its rungs
And they greeted him with divinity and love
There was an air of tranquillity and peace all around
Jacob felt this place was the gateway to heaven
As angels floated 'mongst billowing clouds
And The Lord hovered nigh to his heavenly brethren

The Lord sat beside him and said
I am The Lord and God of thy kin
Abraham and Isaac are but two of the blessed ones
Thou hath been forgiven of thy mortal sin

I wilt give thee and thy descendants this land
They shall be as the dust of the earth
You shall spread abroad north, south, east and west
Thy kin will multiply and give rise to new birth
When Jacob woke from his deep sleep
He said, *Truly The Lord is in this place*
It is none other than the house of God
He felt rejuvenated with a state of grace

Jacob then took the stone on which he'd rested his head
And set it up as a monumental stake
He poured oil over it and called the place Bethal
And promised to be good for The Lord's sake
Jacob continued his journey and came to a land in the east
He noticed flocks of sheep by a deep well
And espied shepherds and enquired about Laban
They replied he was good and as sound as a bell

At that moment Laban's daughter, Rachel arrived
She was herding a flock of Laban's sheep
He approached her and said he was a relative
And indeed did they both kiss and weep

Now Jacob was smitten with Rachel from the start
And he asked Laban for her hand in Marriage
Laban said, First you must work for me for seven years
And thence I shalt prepare a bridal carriage
So Jacob worked seven years for Laban
It seemed but a few days as he loved Rachel so
Then he said to Laban, *Give me my wife*
So I may go to her and make her eyes glow

Now Laban had another daughter named Lia
And she was the elder of the two
But Jacob protested and said to Laban
I worked for thee seven years, now I want what is due
Laban replied, *Complete the week of Lia's nuptials*
For it is not our custom to give Rachel before the first born
Work thee for me another seven years
And Rachel shalt be thy wife I have sworn

Jacob did what he was asked and married Lia
But he went to Rachel whom he loved more
When The Lord saw that Lia was disliked
He made her fruitful and four sons she bore

Meanwhile, Rachel was barren and e'er so sad
She became jealous and gave Jacob, Bala, her maid
She said, *Here is my servant girl for thee to wed*
Jacob married the girl and did as he was bade
Rachel insisted, *Go unto her and lay with her*
So that she may bear on my knees
Then I too will have children by her
To play outside 'mongst fields and trees

And it came to pass that Bala had two sons
And Lia gave Jacob her maid servant too
She also had two boys to become Jacob's heirs
And his eight sons aspired like the morning dew
During the wheat harvest, Ruben found some mandrakes
Rachel asked Lia, *Give some of them to me*
Lia replied, *Is it trivial thou hath taken my husband*
Now thou wanteth my son's mandrake free

Rachel bargained, *Very well! In exchange for the mandrakes*
Thou shalt lie with Jacob tonight
As Jacob returned from the fields, Lia said
This night thou sleeps with me as is my right

Then a miracle came to light
Lisa became fruitful again and conceived
Jacob became the father of ten boys and a girl
He celebrated to The Lord 'mongst rustling leaves
But God remembered Rachel
She bore him a son to Jacob's delight
They called the boy Joseph who was to become a sage
And he filled Jacob's life with sheer delight

The time had come for Jacob to depart to his homeland
And he took with him many animals and fare
He put his family on camels and headed for Chanaan
And he shaded them from the sun's hot glare
Jacob sent forth a message to his brother
As he had to pass through the country of Seir
His messengers returned and gave their report
Esau awaits thee armed with dagger and spear

Jacob sent many gifts from the land
Hoping their friendship could be reconciled
But he need not have worried for The Lord was with him
When he met his brother, Esau sang and smiled

Before he met Esau he sent his family ahead
He could not follow as an angel held him back
The angel informed Jacob that God had changed his name
Henceforth thy name is Israel along God's track
The country of Israel was named after him
As Israel means *Let Got Prevail*
And Jacob became regarded as a patriarch
As his faith in The Lord never again did fail

In a dream, *God appeared again to Jacob*
Go again to Bethal, the place where I spoke to thee
Get rid of all false gods and purify thyself
Change thy clothes and build an altar there for me
On their tedious journey from Bethal to Chanaan
Rachel gave birth to a son in great pain
The deliverance was complicated and difficult
And despite care and attention, Rachel died in vain

Jacob now had twelve sons to his name
And there were twelve tribes of Israel in all
Each son became a father to one tribe
And their names stood out proudly, firm and tall

JOSEPH

Joseph was the youngest of eleven brothers
And Jacob, his father loved him so
His brothers became extremely envious
As Joseph made his father's eyes a glow
The reason why Jacob. loved Joseph the best
'Twas because he became his dad in old age
No happier man, north south, east or west
Also Joseph's nature likened to an aromatic sage

Jacob made him a bright colourful cloak
And his brothers were woeful and sad
And because Joseph did sincerely invoke
They planned to do something bad
Joseph told his brothers about a strange dream
'Twas about each one of them binding sheaves
Mine grew tall, strong and stout
Whereas yours bowed to mine like wilting leaves

Joseph had another dream he did tell
The sun, moon and eleven stars worshipped him it did seem
A reprove to him Jacob did spell
And asked him not to dwell on such a dream

Joseph's brothers were attending their flocks
And Jacob asked Joseph to go and help them
So off he went and walked o'er mud, sand and rocks
Until he eventually came across his brotherly men
When his brothers espied him they became ill at ease
And they plotted to kill him in a devious way
Joseph was happy to see them and e'er so pleased
Quite unaware of what they schemed for him this day

Ruben didn't like what the others did intend
And persuaded them to throw him into a cistern instead
His intent was to save his brother and friend
And to return him to his father's good stead
When along came a caravan Juda had a thought
To sell Joseph to the men from the west
So for twenty pieces of silver, Joseph was bought
And he disappeared o'er a steep sandy crest

Joseph's brothers had his tunic soaked in blood
From a goat that they had just slain
They returned it to Jacob as fast as they could
Lying, they'd tried to save him from a wild animal in vain

The land of Egypt was to be Joseph's fate
And his new master treated him well
Until his wife accused Joseph with a lie
And he ended locked up in a deep prison cell
Now Joseph was well formed and handsome
His master's wife cast her eyes and said
Come hither Joseph and lie with me
But Joseph would not betray his master's stead

Has he fled away she beheld his garment
Then she accused him of wanting to take her
Her husband became angry and grieved
Not realising what really didst occur
Joseph's master committed him to a prison cell
'Twas a deep dungeon place within the prison's wall
But the warden took kindly to Joseph and treated him well
And he placed him in charge of every prisoner's call

There was a butler and a baker as well as him
And each one had a strange dream
Joseph interpreted each dream not on a whim
And both prophesies were correct it did seem

The butler was one of Pharaoh's aids
And he received his freedom and a higher rank
For his freedom and good fortune
He aught to have given Joseph his thanks
Pharaoh, the greatest ruler in the land
Had a most unpredictable dream with a sting
All the learned masters under his command
Couldn't come up with an understandable thing

Twas then the butler recalled Joseph's aid
And he bowed at Pharaoh's feet
He related the prophesy that Joseph had made
And stressed ... 'twas a magical feat
So the lord of a great prosperous nation
Had Joseph brought from a deep dungeon cell
And asked him to interpret in his station
And unveil his dream's deep rooted spell

Seven sleek healthy cows by the Nile
Happily grazed in a field of grass
Seven scrawny cows appeared in a while
And devoured them with ferocious wrath

Seven young sleek healthy cattle
Represented seven years of prosperity and wealth
Whereas seven scrawny ones constituted a battle
Seven years of famine, want and ill health
Joseph's prediction came to the fore
Seven good years of fine wheat and grain a plenty
Pharaoh wisely conserved food into a sealable store
To feed his nation ... both the poor and the gentry

Pharaoh was so pleased with Joseph's deeds
That he placed him at the top of his helm
He knew if he hadn't taken heed
Millions would have perished within his realm
Famine swept throughout Egypt and countries afar
They had to trade with Pharaoh and his team
Jacob sent his sons as if guided by a star
And he prayed to God to help his imploring scheme

He sent forth ten sons to Egypt to buy food
With balsam, laudanum, almond and nuts
They carried with them also oil and crude
Stacked on their caravan up to its butts

Joseph's brothers didn't know him at first
And they had to return again and again
When they recognised him they feared the worst
Because of all the affliction, sorrow and pain
But Joseph forgave his brothers of age
And looked down on them with celestial light
Stating they were responsible for his pilgrimage
And his arduous journey and heavenly plight

Joseph then sent for his family
To see Jacob, his father was a sight to behold
He climbed down from his high ranking seat
And caressed Jacob in the midst of his fold
Joseph asked Jacob and his brothers to stay in the land
As five more years of famine was yet to come
Live well here in Egypt ... the land of sand
And Pharaoh wilt reward thee with a heavenly sum

Jacob agreed but on his death bed he asked of one thing
Bury me with my fathers in a cave
'Tis in a field of Ephron where the angels sing
And 'tis the very last thing for which I crave

Joseph abided by his father's last request
And when he arrived at Goren-Atad
He laid his father Jacob in his chosen place of rest
Then held a great lamentation e'er so sincere and sad
Joseph remained in Egypt with the rest of his family
He lived to an age of one-hundred and ten years
When he died all his brothers prayed on bended knee
And every eye was filled with sadness and tears

MOSES

For Joseph and all of his brothers
Their time on earth had long passed this day
'Twas a time for lovers and mothers
To be fertile happy and gay
The Israelites were fruitful with prolific profuse
They became plentiful like grains of sand
A new king became afraid and obtuse
And designed a new law throughout the land

Task masters were set up over every tribe
Still the poor people spread and multiplied in raves
Pharaoh didst do as revealed by the scribes
Hence, Israelites were turned into slaves
Life became arduous, cruel and bitter
They'd to slave for endless hours on the land
Their profile took on as a down and out critter
Creating bricks from hay, mud and sand

Pharaoh then made a most evil decree
Every Hebrew born baby boy had to be slain
Women were punished for attempting to flee
Trying to save their baby from inhuman bloodstain

A Levite woman gave birth to a little boy
And she committed an offence 'gainst the law
Into a papyrus basket she put her bundle of joy
And placed it in reeds 'tween a river flow
Pharaoh's daughter came to the river to bathe
Whilst her handmaids walked alongside the river bank
On seeing the child she'd a strong desire to keep it safe
So adopted him and raised him to a higher rank

She loved the child as if he were her own flesh
Daily she adorned his cradle with roses
And because she'd drawn him from river afresh
She decided to give him the name Moses
Moses's life-style was one of fine riches and care
He grew up and became a very strong man
His stepmother loved him so and made him aware
His birthright was not Egyptian but of Hebrew clan.

One day when Moses was visiting his kin
He beheld an Egyptian lashing a Hebrew man
His blood boiled in his veins and he committed a sin
He slew the offender and buried him in sand

To Pharaoh the killing didst come to light
And Moses was thus condemned to die
But Pharaoh then granted a divergent plight
And cast him into the desert so arid and dry
Moses struggled in the wilderness's high winds and sand
Could hardly walk o'er each sand dune's high slope
Until he felt the touch of an angel's hand
And it gave him courage, will, faith and hope

He finally arrived at Midian's well
When seven ladies came to water their flocks by day
Some shepherds came and gave them torment and hell
Moses defended them and drove the herdsmen away
Raguel, their father was happy with life
He invited Moses to stay at his house
He even gave his daughter Sepphora to be his wife
And Moses was happy to take her as his spouse

Said Moses. *I am a stranger in your land*
And yet ye treat me as part of your family
Sepphora bore a son in the country of sand
And he grew up in an aura so loving and free.

A long time passed and Egyptian cruelty didst exist
And God heard all their prayers and groans
So The Lord let Moses know what didst persist
His people cruelly treated from dusk till dawn
Moses was about tending a flock of sheep
When an angel appeared within a burning bush
Despite the flame being e'er so fierce and deep
The thicket remained so vibrant, healthy and lush

God spoke to Moses from within the flame
And bade him return to the place of his birth
His task was for Pharaoh to cease all the pain
And release all slaves to enjoy God's earth
What should I say if they ask me thy name?
To them I'd be like a new born lamb
I am who I am and you will tell them the same
And when they ask who senteth thee tell them 'I Am

How could he do such an incredible thing
He was not learned or eloquent in speech
God replied it was he who gives power to talk and sing
And would implant wisdom enabling Moses to teach

Moses confronted the sovereign in his kingdom great
Pharaoh just laughed and remained calm and cool
To release all the slaves from their impending fate
He waved his arms and called Moses a fool
Moses threw down his staff to the ground
And a large serpent appeared large and brash
Two magicians made two snakes appear around
Moses's creature devoured them both in a flash

Pharaoh was not the least impressed
And declared he would not let the slaves go
Moses replied his kingdom would ne'er be blessed
And further afflictions on his palace would flow
Pharaoh's heart hardened and he took no heed
So followed ten plagues for his lack of love
Blood, frogs, gnats, and flies attacked life giving seeds
Boils, pestilence and hail cast down from above

All of these things didn't soften Pharaoh's heart
And God sent locusts to devour every field
'Twas enough to rip a normal man's brain apart
But not ample to make Pharaoh yield

God then sent a black cloud down on his land
A darkness so dense it could be felt
The Egyptians couldn't make out the shape of a hand
Yet pharaoh's heart failed to submit or melt
For his contumacy God made a another decree
And it brought Pharaoh down to his knees
Leaving him no option but to set the slaves free
To enjoy the gift of a fresh open air breeze

A grey mist wilt pass by and kill every first born
Especially if the child is Egyptian creed
Even the first born animal of any form
Pharaoh's inured heart 'twill wilt and bleed
Blood of lambs sprinkled on house doors
'Twas a sign for the mist to pass by
No one to step outside The Lord above implores
All people within will heed a wailing cry

After the Passover Pharaoh set the slaves free
Into a vast barren desert was their plight
But later he recalled soldiers to bended knee
And charged after the slaves in a raging flight

The Israelites were trapped against the sea
As chariots charged forward in vengeful array
The Lord opened the water to let the slaves flee
Dry land allowed them to go safely on their way
Egyptian chariots followed close on their heels
But the waters closed and swallowed them up
The Israelites now knew how it feels
To be under the protection of God's blessed cup

The Israelites had crossed the Red Sea
From their oppressors they'd finally been freed
But ahead of them lay a barren wilderness
Where danger and famine were constantly at heed
God's deliverance from slavery and other special gifts
Were soon forgotten in the desert's burning heat
Despite witnessing many miracles and blessings
They did naught but complain, whine and bleat

Their grumblings made Moses' task e'er so formidable
And it took a toll on his family and wife
Despite raining manna down from the sky
At times he even feared for his life

In the new land was an air of discontent
As food and water were extremely hard to find
Many leaders grumbled with contempt
Hunger and thirst, despite hard work and grind
So the Lord rained manna and quail down from the sky
And from a large rock, water came a flowing
Small roots and grass plants appeared by and by
Also other gifts to keep the camp up and a glowing

God then called upon Moses from way up high
And commanded him to climb Sinai's mountain path
Ten commandments in stone!" was a high pitched cry
To be obeyed truly or wreak my wrath!
But when Moses' absence was prolonged
The Israelites became agitated once again
They approached Aaron to make a golden calf
Which caused God heartache and pain

When Moses retuned from the mount
He was carrying two tablets of stone
On them were written the Ten Commandments
For all mankind to keep and atone

However, when Moses espied the golden calf
His anger flared up with all of his wrath
And he cast the stones at the Israelites
And they smashed to pieces on the mountain path
Moses realised what he had just done
And he knelt down and prayed fervently on his knees
He asked The Lord for wisdom during a setting sun
And how to deal with their sin and terrible decrees

The Lord reproached Moses for his moment of wrath
By the slightest movement of his hand
Moses was allowed to carry on his heavenly path
But was banned from entering The Promised Land
Forty more years the Israelites endured the desert sand
Before they set eyes on the land to the east
'Twas a sight so welcoming and grand
They all sat down to a celebratory ` feast

Moses kept the promise to God he had made
Forty years had the Israelites survived in desert sand,
Finally he arrived at an extraordinary scenic glade
The place he had assured ... near to The Promised Land.

Then Moses moved to Moab near Mount Nebo
And the Lord showed him the Promised Land
He scanned the place as far as Segor
This is the land I swore to Abraham and his clan
I have let thee feast thy eyes upon it
But thou shalt not cross over to the other side
So gather together thy belongings and kit
For in the land of Moab thou shalt bide

Later, Moses died and was buried in a ravine
'Twas in the boundary of Moab land
And no more was he ever seen
As his grave was covered with stormy sand

Moses was one-hundred and twenty years old when he died.

THE TEN COMMANDMENTS

At Mount Sinai God gave the Israelites an unparalleled gift
He gave them the Ten Commandments written in stone
The ten laws had to be obeyed without waver or drift
None to be broken lest thou should atone
The commands were spiritual ... a guidance for man
Words of wisdom and truth ordained by the one most high
To keep on the right path, God's divine plan
A precious treasure from a heavenly sky
The Ten Commandments are a spiritual law
That existed long before man inhabited the earth
Keep them with integrity and thy life shall flow
Forsake them and a man's souls forsakes its worth
Abide by the holy laws and live blessed and well
'Twill bring dazzling gifts into thriving lives
Disobey them and add flames to the fires of hell
And cause nothing but dread and distressed lives

JOSUA

After Moses died Josua became leader of his clan
God appeared to him in a dream and spoke
He made it clear the way of his heavenly plan
And how Josua must be true and daily invoke

"Prepare thyself to cross the River Jordon here
And guide all thy people to the Promised Land
I wilt deliver to thee every place thou sets near
Whether it be fertile soil or desert sand

Your domain shalt be cities and great places
I will watch over thee in ferocious fights
Thou shalt overcome many fierce tribes and races
And thy people wilt dwell in prosperous sites
Be firm and stout and abide by my laws
Do not stray either to the left or to the right
Be faithful and succeed wherever you go
Keep my commandments and be pleasing in my sight"

Josua did as what The Lord had bade
He stressed on the Israelites all of God's laws
They kept to God's words and their loyalty paid
Under the guidance of God, they defeated their foes

Henceforth, Josua sent two agents to seek how the land lies
And they lodged in a harlot's place
But the king became aware of the two spies
And he descended on her home in furious pace
Rahab was her name and she lied through her teeth
She said they had been there but had left the same day
She pointed to in the direction of the desert with grief
And stressed that by now they were well on their way

Rahab had hidden the two men in the roof space
And concealed them amongst stalks of flax
The plants grew thickly in a darkened space
Hiding both of them and covering their backs
Before they fell asleep, Rahab approached them and made a plea
As she had heard of the power of Josua's God
His reputation had spread o'er land and sea
And she feared the pain of His heavenly rod

She was aware that God had opened the Red Sea
As were all of the inhabitants of the city
The way the Israelites brought kings to bended knee
And doomed them to destruction without mercy or pity

She begged them to have pity on her and her clan
And to give her an unmistakeable token
A symbol that would save her siblings, her dad and mam
The spies agreed to this and a promise was spoken
They pledged their lives if Rahab protected them so
And she didn't betray this awesome task
She then informed them where to hide from her foe
Up in mountainous country where the could rest and bask

She let them down from an elevated room
With a rope down the side of a high city wall
They advised her to use the scarlet cord as a bloom
To advise soldiers not to harm her house at all
To let the scarlet cord dangle from the windowsill
And to gather all her family into her house
Advise everyone to remain quiet and still
And all will be well with your siblings and spouse

The two agents escaped across the River Jordon back to base
They assured Josua that's Jericho's people
were filled with fear
Josua moved his troops to lodge by the river face
Each geared up in armour with sword, knife and spear

Josua issued orders given to him by The Lord
To follow the Ark of the Covenant from behind
They then were protected by God's blessed word
And victory was theirs in body and mind
He promised they would witness wonders the next day
And every Israelite was filled with confidence and joy
They rejoiced near to camp-fires happy and gay
As they all were hopeful in The Lord's ploy

Next day priests carried The Covenant to the river's bank
And as soon as they entered the water with their feet
The River Jordon ceased to flow normally in rank
And backed upstream in a miraculous feat
Water dispersed and the riverbed became solid ground
Making it easy for the priests and others to cross
All the soldiers marched forward homeward bound
Unencumbered they moved swiftly without any time loss

About forty-thousand soldiers crossed the river
The Lord exalted Josua in front of his men
Thenceforth they respected him as a spiritual giver
And like Moses, he was officiated by the stroke of a pen

As the priests carrying the Ark ascended to dry land
The waters of the Jordon resumed their course
And the banks overflowed everywhere around
As water roared furiously from every source
After the crossing, Josua chose twelve strong men
And he ordered each one to lift up a large river stone
Each stone was to represent a memorial gem
Where the priests last stood in the river zone

The stones would remind generations to come
When the waters of the Jordon ceased to flow
When the miracle struck the Israelites numb
And filled their enemies with dismay and woe
The city of Jericho was in a state of siege
None of its people could either enter or leave.
The air was hot with hardly a breeze
Making it hard for the citizens to breathe

Priests took up the Ark of The Lord
And seven walked around the city blowing ram's horns
Picked troops marched ahead as ordered by word
And rear guards followed bearing daggers and thorns

The priests continuously blew the horns on the march
On the seventh day they walked around the city seven times
Their enemies cringed within the castles arch
'Twas a celestial stage in biblical thymes
Josua commanded his people not to shout
And to remain quiet until he gave the order
Only after the seventh march did it come about
And loud boisterous voices rang out from border to border

The strong vibrations caused the Jericho's walls to fall
And the army stormed the city in frontal attack
They killed every living creature within the wall
Men, women, young and old lay dead on their back
But Rahab, the harlot and family were spared
The promise the agent's made her rang true
Because Rehab had hidden the agents and cared
She and her family received their life that was due

Josua went on to defeat more cities and kings
As he constantly remained true to God
The Lord displayed his loyalty in miraculous ways
As the Israelites conquered wherever they trod

Gabaon formed a coalition with Israel's band
So five Amorrite kings united en-mas
Their plan was to wipe out Gabaon from the land
But they hadn't taken into account Josua's brash
An Israeli army marched against the Amorrites
And inflicted great slaughter amongst them all
God remained with them in all their fights
And many thousands of Amorrites did falter and fall

As many Amorrites fled from the battle scene
Thousands were killed by large hailstones from the sky
'Twas as bloody a massacre as ever as been
Throughout the land resounded a loud victory cry
Meanwhile the five kings fled and hid in a cave
But their hideout was discovered by and by
And a great stone was rolled in front by soldiers brave
The kings were trapped and surely would die

After the battle, Josua opened the cave
Soldiers forced the kings to their knees
Then Josua, to his soldiers, orders he gave
The kings were hung on five glorious trees

They were left hanging there until sunset
And were then cast into the cave where they'd hidden
Josua felt that now they'd repaid their debt
And that he had fulfilled The Lord's bidding
Over the mouth of the cave, the large stones were replaced
And they remain there until this day
A warning that human kind should not be defaced
As man is meant to live a life happy and gay

Josua lived to be 110 years old

DANIEL

Brothers Daniel, Ananias, Misael and Azarias
Were the wisest four in all the land
But to Daniel also was given understanding
From God above with the touch of his hand
Daniel was able to interpret dreams and visions
Of prosperity, famine and things yet to come
The king of Babylon who ruled o'er provisions
Summoned Daniel to be transformed to his Kingdom

The king of Babylon had a strange dream
And even though it was fearsome, no doubt
Try as he would through strife and steam
He couldn't recall what his vision was about
To all the wise-men an urgent message was sent
Commanded to bring his dream to the fore
And to interpret what the inspiration meant
To most men ... an impossible chore

All the intellectuals beget a petrified state
Failure meant they were sentenced to death
For the masters 'twas an act of ill fate
As they were about to take their last breathe

Daniel was then summoned to the king
And he was able the bring the dream alive
The answer came as an angel did sing
He and his brothers did up and thrive
A tall statue with a head of gold
Silver kept the breasts and arms at bay
Belly and thighs of brass did unfold
And the feet were made of iron and clay

A colossal stone was cut from a mountain pass
And it struck the figurine's feet
The entire statue smashed into tiny pieces of chaff
And were scattered north, west, south and east
The gigantic stone became a great mountain
And it covered the entire earth
A holy reign appeared as a fountain
And God reigned superb with all His worth

The statue represented kingdoms torn apart
Crumbling due to cruelty, unfairness and greed
God intervened and made a new start
And took over by heavenly creed

God hath shown what will come to pass
He'll set up his kingdom of purity and love
It'll shine and sparkle like crystalline glass
'Twill forever radiate in the heavens above
Against God's kingdom nought shall prevail
And his authority will rule o'er sky, land and sea
His promise is the start of a beautiful tale
His realm will prevail for all eternity

The king then built an enormous statue of gold
"Twas sixty cubits high and six cubits wide
Symphony and psaltery of music did unfold
He then summoned all subjects to his side
The king pointed to the sculpture and raised his hand
And he gave an order that it had to be adorned
Daniel refused to abide by the law of the land
And by the king's wise-men was immorally scorned

Sidrach, Misach and Abderago, three sages
Also disobeyed and slighted the King's decree
Like all evil kings throughout the ages
He condemned them to die, all three

The holy sages were cast within a furnace
But as the oven was tuned way up high
An angelic expression radiated on each face
As they were sentenced to suffer and die
The furnace burnt at its highest degree
But the flames ne'er touched a hair on each head
As they floated amidst the heat happy and free
The coals flared with cinders fiery red

The king liked Daniel and wanted to let it go
But he was approached by the learned men
And they convinced him Daniel was indeed a foe
He was condemned and cast into a lions' den
Daniel thrived in the den for six days
Amongst seven ferocious wild beasts
Habacus, a prophet, was carried by an angel in praise
To bring for Daniel a ravishing feast

The scribes had schemed and kept the lions hungry
The fierce cats purred and made David a friend
Normally the wild beasts would devour all and sundry
'Twas something divergent … 'twas a mystical trend

For their deviousness, corruption and lies
The learned scribes were tried from the heart
And far away were heard all their cries
As ferocious lions ripped and tore them apart
The king sawest all that had occurred
And he acknowledged Daniel's God henceforth
From thence he was true to his word
And praised the Lord with all of his worth

Daniel in his time had many more missions
Of things in life yet to come
And he interpreted scores of visions
Of God and His heavenly kingdom

ESTHER

King Asseurus ruled over many providences in a vast land
And Susan was the name of his capital city
He ruled over his people by a slight touch of his hand
His reign was built upon wisdom, fairness and piety
Alas he loved to boast of his great holdings and wealth
And he threw a magnificent banquet for kings near and far
'Twas not a good ingredient for sanity and health
As wealth cannot buy friendship nor keep a mind wise and ajar

Many kings arrived and enjoyed the awesome splendour
As did princes and lords from far off lands
Alas, the royal occasion lacked that special glow
As Queen Vasthi cast a desert into blistering sands
Queen Vasthi refused to attend the feast
And made the king feel way down low
He felt humiliated in front of fine gentry fro' west and east.
For her conduct he created a new law

He made a decree that all wives must honour their spouse

A law was set up in each and every aden
Queen Vasthi was barred form the king's house
And replaced by a most beautiful virgin maiden

Esther had been raised by Mardochai who's abode was at the king's gate
She was exceedingly fair and amiable in the eyes of all
She was pleasing in the king's eyes and it became
her heavenly fate
Esther was to become queen during a most prestigious ball
At the king's gate, Mardochai became aware of a plot against the throne
He informed Esther and bade her to relate it to the king
This she did via a high ranking officer's pawn
Who hence informed the king of a terrible thing

Two Eunochs had connived a treacherous plot
And both were hanged on a wooden gibbet high
To be found guilty was their blessed fate
And they were sentenced to death by and by
However Aman, a high ranking officer took credit for everything
And for his guile he was promoted to the highest rank
All servants bent their knees as he was now second

only to the king
All bowed except Mardochai who was aware of
Aman's devious prank

Aman detested Mardochai and made a plot to kill him
He knew Mardochai was of Jewish race
He approached the king and lied that all Jews detested his laws on a whim
A command was proclaimed to kill every Jew at a furious pace

A decree was posted on every post and fence
That every Jew, old and young, had to be slain
The poor Jews had no way of self-defence
And they clambered and cried out in pain
Also a decree was set up by the royal scribes
In diverse languages it was written and sent
The order to reach many kingdoms and tribes
And rent a danger to Jews wherever it was sent

Now Mardochai knew he had to do something fast
And he bade Esther to sit by his side
To her he requested a most dangerous task
As she was about to become the king's bride
For a strict law from way back in time

'Twas written in the archives and set in stone
Without permission from the king's thyme,
No one to enter the chamber of the king's throne

To enter without permission was a grievous deed
To do so was under the threat of death
If a soul happened to do so without heed
No clemency from the king they took their last breathe

Esther listened ardently but then became afraid
She was in her prime and feared for her life
As would be the state of any young maid
Despite knowing she was about to become the king's wife
Think not that thou mayest save thy life only," Mardochai bade
Think also of all thy kinfolk, both home and away
So Esther, though nervous and terribly afraid
Went forward into the king's chamber to cower and pray

On entering she was arrested by the king's guard
But the king raised his sceptre allowing her through
He allowed her clemency by the sign of a ring
Claiming she was so special, one of a few
The king was smitten and loved Esther so
To thee thou canst have half my kingdom and more

Make to me thy plea and it wilt make my heart glow
For thee I wilt cast open any door

Esther requested a banquet e'er so divine
Special guests were for just Aman, herself and the king
Aman was pleased as it suited him fine
As it appeared to place him like a bird on the wing

Just prior to this, Aman had ordered his henchmen
To build a gibbet over 80 cubits high
His evil plot to hang Mardochai by the stroke of a pen
On the gibbet the sage would suffer and die
But to Aman's surprise during the magnificent feast
Esther disclosed to the king Aman's devious plot
And the evil doings of the bestial beast
Hence, the plot to hang Mardochai became Aman's lot

Now in turn, Mardochai was raised way up high
And Aman's evil decree was turned around
The Israelites prayers were answered from a star
And The Lord blessed the Jews with holy fertile land

JOB

In the land of Ur lived an upright, blameless man
His name was Job and he feared The Lord
Seven sons and seven daughters were of his clan
Many sheep, oxen, camels asses were in his hoard
He was wealthier than any man in the east
And all his children were happy and content
His sons oft' put on a glorious feast
And they lived in harmony with Job's consent

One day whilst rejoicing, Satan arrived on the scene
And The Lord asked, *From whence do you come*
His reply was from roaming the earth wherever he'd been
And he'd noticed Job was a special chum
That's because he is good and avoids everything bad
Thou shalt not find any evil in him
Saturn scorned and pointed out everything that Job had
Stating he would sin if things turned out more grim

Satan replied, *Is it for nothing that Job feareth thee*
Thou hast surrounded him with family and wealth

You've adorned him and blessed his family tree
And everything he has is full of vitality and health

Touch anything of Job's and he will blaspheme thee
And he will sin like any other clan
The Lord answered, *Behold it in your power to see*
But lay not a hand upon the man
So Satan went about his evil deed
And he brought disaster onto Job's life
First a vicious mob stole all his animals and creed
Causing Job and his family lots of grief and strife

Then a great wind blew o'er desert land
And smote the four corners of Job's house
It fell upon all his children and band
All were killed except for his loving spouse
Then Job began to tear his cloak and cut off his hair
He cast himself prostrate on the ground
I came forth from my mother's womb naked and bare
But a word of malice he uttered not a sound

Once again Satan came along
And The Lord said *From whence did you come*
And Satan answered with a smooth silver tongue

I still feel Job is a special chum

All that thou hast taken from this man
Which I allowed thee to do without cause
He still holds fast and true despite your evil plan
And his faith in The Lord is still on course
And Satan answered, Skin for skin
All that a man has he will give for his life
Put forth thy hand and touch his bone and shin
And he will surely blaspheme thee with might and strife

And The Lord gave Satan another quote
He is in thy power: only spare his life
So Satan departed into a bottomless moat
And caused poor Job more tribulations and strife
He smote Job with severe boils and ills
From the soles of his feet to the crown of his head
Job had to cleanse himself with pots-head that chills
And it made him feel he'd be better off dead

Job's wife was devastated and told him so
Why don't you curse God and die
Job replied, Why do you speak as senseless women do

We except good things from God ... why not evil by and by

Now three friends heard of Job's pain
They wanted to help him in his distress
To give him comfort 'twas a journey in vain
'Twas a problem they knew not how to address
When they espied him with anguish in their eyes
They did not recognise him and began to weep
They threw of their cloaks 'neath clouded skies
For his suffering was so vile and deep

They sat with him for seven nights
But not one of them spoke a word to him
'Neath a star laden sky filled with brilliant lights
They felt his anguish so painful and grim
Then Job opened his mouth and spoke with fire
Why did The Lord allow me to suck at the breasts'
If not I would have been certain to expire
And now be laden in heavenly rest

Perish the day on which I was born
On the night when informed the child is a boy
For now I feel nought but grief and forlorn

Gone is my feeling of happiness and joy

Job was so full of anguish and rage
He didn't realise what he was saying
But then he returned to his typical stage
Hence he knelt down and did a lot of praying
I know O Lord thou can do all things
Therefore I lament and cast my words into dust and ashes
I look forward to listening as a skylark sings
And discard my loose tongue with whips and lashes

The Lord accepted Job's intercession with delight
And he restored his health, all his possession and more
Job's life once again became happy and bright
As he could help the downcast and the poor
The Lord blessed Job's latter days
With another seven sons and three daughters
His daughters 'ere so beautiful in many ways
His life serene and deep like still waters

Job lived to be one-hundred and forty years of age
And he saw his grandchildren and more

Now free from the terrible pestilient stage
He gave each an inheritance from his worldly store.

SAMSON AND DELILAH

At one time the Israelites offended The Lord
And he punished them and brought fourth tears
He delivered them into the hands of their enemies
And the Philistines ruled them for forty years
There was a certain man from Saraa
He was a Danite and Manoe was his name
His wife was barren and had no children
But to her an angel of The Lord came

Though thou art barren and have no children
Yet thou wilt conceive and bear a baby boy
Take no wine or eat anything unclean
And the child will fill thy heart with joy
As for the son he will grow big and powerful
Take care not to let a razor touch his head
The boy is to be consecrated by God from the womb
He wilt deliver thee from the Philitine's stead

Manoe knelt down and prayed fervently
O Lord my God in heaven I beseech thee

My wife and I know not what to do
Please teach us and open our eyes to see

And it came to pass that the woman bore a son
The boy grew fast and Samson was his name
When a man he went into town and espied a Philistine woman
And this was to cause havoc in the hall of fame
On return home to his parents he told them
There is a woman in Thamna whom I wish to wed
They were concerned as she was a Philistine
As they preferred he marry a local girl instead

But Samson insisted and said to his father
Do as I say father, for she pleases me
There was no changing of Samson's mind
No matter how hard his parent's did plea
So Samson went down into Thamna
Hand in hand with his father and mother
At the vineyards a young lion came charging close
And Samson's parents had no sign of cover

Samson had no weapon but he tore the lion in pieces
And a large crowd who espied the awesome feat
Was amazed by his incredible strength

But the Philistines smirked and called him a cheat

Later when Samson returned to marry the maid
He stopped to look at the remains of the beast
He spotted a swarm of bees and lots of honey
'Twas enough sweetness to enhance a prince's feast
Thirty Philistines attended Samson's wedding
And he proposed a riddle to each of them
It you solve it within seven days
To each one I wilt give a tunic with a hem

If thou doth not solve the riddle
Each one of you gives a tunic to me
Everyone of them gloated and laughed
Propose thy riddle, one said, *we will listen to thee*
Samson smiled and then quoted the riddle
Out of the eater came forth food
And out of the strong came sweetness
It turned the Philistines into a sombre mood

After three days they'd failed to resolve it
On the fourth day they threatened Samson's wife
Coerce thy husband to give us the answer

Or so help us it wilt cost thee thy life

Unwillingly she coerced the answer from Samson
And she gave it to her country men
They couldn't wait to see Samson's face
As they laughed and solved it there and then
The devious band had purposely waited a while
On the seventh day just before the sun had set
What is sweeter than honey or stronger than a lion
Samson was outraged knowing he'd lost his bet

Samson went down to down to Ascolon
Where he killed thirty of their men
He despoiled them and took their garments
And cast them within the cheater's den
However, disarray and fighting broke out
And they threatened to take Samson's life
But during the terrible turmoil
The rebels finished up killing Samson's wife

From thence, Samson became a fugitive
And he caused the Philistines sorrow and pain
He hunted and caught three-hundred foxes

And used them to set fire to fields of grain

He also destroyed vineyards and olive orchards
And inflicted a great slaughter on their men
Samson's own people asked why he did this
As it brought trouble down onto them
They said, *We have come to take thee prisoner*
We wilt bind thee and take you to the Philistines
We promise that we wilt not kill thee
But the enemy's wrath is great for killing their vines

Unbeknown to his clan, soldiers lay waiting in ambush
When Samson espied them he picked up the jawbone of an ass
In a ravine formed from granite and stone
And slew one-thousand Philistines with ferocious brass
Samson was now a most wanted outlaw
And he had to live alone in a cave
He was unhappy and fled to another region
Where there was a woman for whom he didst crave

Samson in his loneliness met a lady named Delilah
And something about her touched his heart

She was not only beautiful but clever and astute
He fell in love with her from the very start

Delilah loved Samson but she betrayed him for money
Philistines offered her gold and she plainly agreed
They wanted to know the secret of Samson's strength
And she succumbed to their offer in a state of greed
Samson was infatuated with Delilah's beauty and allure
Not realising she was devious and sly
Her beauty veiled a heart made of stone
She connived and Samson's end drew nigh

Delilah with love, tenderness and soothing words
Sought to unravel the secret of his power
When she realised it lie within his hair
She cut off his locks like pruning a flower
His enemies then descended on upon him
And he was as weak as any ordinary man
They gouged out his eyes and blinded him
And cast into a dungeon with a lifetime ban

The lords of Philistine praised their god Dagon
For Dagon had delivered Samson into their hands

They dragged Samson into the temple's arena
And celebrated with jeers and musical bands

They scourged Samson and tormented him
But he played the buffoon in front of the crowd
Unbeknown to them his strength had returned
Despite his fate he stood firm and proud
After torturing and causing lots of pain
They placed Samson between two pillars tall
The pillars were the main bearers of the temple
Should they collapse the temple would fall

Samson cried out to The Lord and said
O Lord God remember me, strengthen me
O God, for the last time I may avenge myself
And die along with the Philistines for thee
Samson called upon God and his call was answered
He pushed hard against the pillars and beheld a rumble
The pillars crashed down with tons of stone
Thousands were killed as the temple didst tumble

All his family went to the site to collect Samson's remains
And he was laid near to his father's head

His named was recalled by the holy scribes
And his story will be passed down and read

RUTH

At one time there was a famine in Juda
So a man from Bethlehem departed with his family
His wife and two sons were by his side
He took them to Moab, a land open and free
The man was kind and his name was Elimelech
And Noemi was the name of his wife
Shortly after reaching the Moabite plateau
Both sons married and swore an allegiance for life

Things were fine and then tragedy struck
Noemi's husband and two sons suddenly died
She was devastated by the loss of her family
But with her misfortune she had to abide
Word reached her that God had given Juda food
Hence, she and her two sister's in law left the place
The two in-laws were called Orpha and Ruth
And all three set off in a state of grace

But when they were on the road back to Juda

Noemi said to her daughter's-in-law
Return each of you to thy mother's house
For I don't want to see thee full of sorrow and woe

Orpha kissed her mother-in-law goodbye
But Ruth refused and stayed by Noemi's side
Ruth said *Wherever thou goes I goest too*
Both women sat down and openly cried
So they travelled together and reached Juda
And Ruth worked arduously in the fields with care
Booz, the landowner, took note of her plight
As she struggled on in weather windy and fair

Booz was kind to Ruth and earned her respect
But her dedication to Naomi never waned
She trusted Naomi with her life
And her loyalty and faithfulness remained
Booz was impressed and asked who the girl was
The overseer stated she was of Moabite clan
She arrived here from the plateau with Naomi
And works as hard as a young strong man

She asked leave to gather the gleanings into sheaves
And for hours she works hard along with the rest

She arrived early this morning and up until now
She has scarcely stopped for a moment's rest

Booz said to Ruth *Listen my friend*
Do not glean in any one else's fields
Stay here with my women servants
And watch carefully as the harvest yields
I have commanded the men to do thee no harm
When thou art thirsty, from our vessels thou may drink
Ruth was grateful and cast herself prostrate on the ground
Her respect for Booz now at its highest link

At mealtime Booz approached Ruth and said
Come hither to me and take food to eat
Drink well and dip thy bread in the sauce
She ate roasted grain and found it nice and sweet
Booz instructed his servants to let Ruth glean the sheaves
And he allowed her to glean from the earth
And it came to about an epha of barley
Which she took home to Naomi with all its worth

It became obvious to every one around
That Ruth and Booz were smitten with each other

Gradually they became a courting couple
And Ruth became Booz's lover

They courted for just a little while
Then Booz took Ruth to be his bride
The Lord above blessed their marriage
And they lived constantly side by side
When they came together as man and wife
She became with child and bore Booz a son
Ruth took the child upon her knee
And together they created lots of love and fun

Time passed and the boy became a man
He married and begat a son called Obed
Obed also grew and became a man
He married and his wife bore Jesse in stead
Finally Jesse was to become the father of David
And David was to rule as a king
He became renowned for his music and songs
And the way he slew Goliath with a stone and a sling

SAMUEL

Elcana, the son of Jeroham, lived in Solo
He had two wives named Phenenna and Anna to wit
Phenenna had two sons to her husband
Whereas Anna was barren as in the scrolls it was writ
Anna was sad and forlorn as she so wanted to be with child
And she prayed ardently to The Lord from her heart
Heli, a high priest thought she was drunk
For as her lips moved, not a sound wouldst depart

The Lord maketh the poor and He maketh the rich
He humbleth and He exalteth each soul
Her husband Elcana knew Anna and she conceived
She gave birth to a boy by her heavenly call
After Anna had weaned the child she praised The Lord
She took offerings to the house of God in Silo
She thanked Him ardently for hearing her prayer
And henceforth blessings of Samuel didst flow

She named the child Samuel and he was so special indeed

Samuel grew and The Lord was by his side
He lived by the commandments of The Lord
Throughout his life by the words of God didst he abide

Samuel grew and The Lord was with him
And not one of his words fell to the ground
The lord blessed him and it came to pass
His words of wisdom were solid and sound
From a young age he served in the temple
His heart was openly pure and bright
He brought hope to Israel's people
And helped them in their troublesome plight

All the people were impressed by his deeds
And they wished him to rule over every thing
They raised him up to a to a high ranking place
And hailed him like a reigning king
But the people were restless and worshipped false gods
They were unhappy with life and their fate
They were under the whip of the Philistines
And were treated as servants with an air of hate

Many more people departed from the good path
And they broke the commandments of God

They committed adultery amongst other things
And refused to abide by The Lord's guiding rod

The Israelites were ruled by the Philistines
And had to abide by their laws
They appealed to Samuel to help them
But he came up with a biblical clause
The Lord thy God has forsaken thee
Because thou hast adorned false gods and sinned
He has turned his back against you
And cast thee against fierce blustery winds

So Samuel made it clear to the Israelites
If you pray to The lord with a sincere heart
And put away from thee all false gods
Then from thy land thy Philistines shalt depart
To win thyself God's love and blessings
Thou needs to kneel down and repent
Henceforth, the Lord wilt forgive thee
And his blessings will be heavenly sent

The Israelites did what Samuel asked of them

And they cast aside all false gods and sincerely didst repent
They knelt and begged for forgiveness
The Lord was happy and didst relent

Once again the Philistines started to battle
But for them it was a tactical blunder
As this time God was with the Israelites
And they conquered with lightning and thunder
Samuel ruled over Israel for the rest of his life
And the lives of all were happy and content
As peace and happiness dwelt in their homes
Like the Garden of Eden 'twas Godly sent

The Israelites were happy under Samuel's rule
But when he was old, feeble and frail
He appointed his two sons to take charge
But it was a choice destined to fail
Samuel's two sons walked not in his ways
And they lived as in a charlatan like ring
The people appealed against Samuel's choice
And requested they be ruled instead by a king

So Samuel knelt and prayed to the Lord
And he spoketh to Him of Israel's plea
The Lord replied, *Listen to them, give them what they ask*
And I wilt find an upright king for thee

Hearken to my voice for tomorrow at this time
I wilt send thee a man of mine own choice
He will be in the town square with other men
Listen carefully and take heed of my voice
The man is called Saul and he is the son of Cis
Saul is a good man and respected by all
His father's asses have strayed and got lost
To find them he hath called upon Saul

So next day Samuel went to the square
And he was approached by a handsome looking gent
And when Samuel set eyes on him
He knew he was the man whom God had sent
Saul was tall and handsome with a noble face
And he appeared to answer Israel's prayer
Samuel studied and espied him from afar
And felt a sense of a kingly air

Saul approached Samuel in the midst of the square
He asked, *Tell me please, where is the house of the seer*
Samuel replied, *I am he, come with me to the high place*
All will be revealed to thee ... a special pier

Fear not for thy father's asses, they have been found
The Lord has revealed this to me
Also that you are about to be crowned king
'Tis a heavenly message from God to thee
But I an but a humble shepherd, replied Saul
I have just a simple crook to guide my sheep
Am I not of the least tribe of Israel
Why doth thou put a throne within my keep?

Samuel answered and put Saul at ease
It is not I but God who has chosen thy fate
So think not of the reason why
'Tis a spiritual message from heaven's gate
Samuel then took a little vial of oil
And with it he poured a little onto Saul's head
Behold The Lord hath anointed thee
And thou shalt be king in the Lord's stead

Immediately, the whole of Saul's countenance changed
God gave unto him another heart that day
And so it came to pass as decreed
Saul's life path was set down a different way

All of the people he had known were taken aback
What is this that has happened to the son of Cis
Is Saul also amongst the holy prophets
His facial expression is of heavenly bliss
Samuel consulted all of the people and said
This man has been chosen by God ... rejoice and sing
There is none other like him to rule in stead
All the people rejoiced and sang, *May God save the king*

KING SAUL

Saul was chosen by God to lead his people
And he was the first king of Israel's land
Tall, strong and handsome with a kingly air
His life to reign began e'er so grand
And it came to pass that a war broke out
Naas, an Ammonite came to fight on the land
The Israelites wanted to make a covenant to serve
But Naas stressed it would be under his command

Naas agreed to a covenant on one condition
That he pluck out the right eye of every Israelite clan
The people were devastated by Naas' decree
And they made Saul aware of the evil plan
Saul thought long and hard and ardently prayed
And the spirit of The Lord came upon him
He gathered and spoke to the people in great array
And he slew the Ammonites in a battle so grim

And Saul, having his kingdom established
He fought against many enemies thereabout
Against Moab, the Philistines and whithersoever
And defeated them fiercely without any doubt

All the Israelite people loved Saul
And this made Saul's ego swell with pride
And he tended to turn away from the Lord
And his change of heart was noted far and wide
Samuel noticed and went to reprove Saul
Thou hast been foolish and disobeyed God's command
For this thy kingdom shalt not continue
Behold a young boy named David shalt take over thy hand

Jealousy consumed Saul and hatred entered his mind
But future years saw David rise to a high place
For Saul, the king had lost his way
His legacy tarnished through lack of grace
Saul was determined to kill David
And he chased him across mountains and land
But David remained faithful and true to The Lord
Despite Saul striving to kill him with a ruthless band

Sadly, Saul'end came in battle with the Philistines
His three sons were slain in the war against Saul
Saul was grievously injured by an archer's arrow
Which caused him to stumble and fall

Then Saul pleaded with his armour bearer
Draw thy sword and kill me I pray thee
For I do not want to fall into the philistines' hands
But the armour bearer refused Saul's pitiful plea
Hence, Saul took his sword and fell upon it
And when his armour bearer saw this to wit
That Saul was dead he also did the same
And both their lives were no longer lit

So on that day Saul and his three sons died
And the armour bearer and all of his men
They all perished in battle together
As was written by the stroke of a pen
The rise and fall of Saul is plain to see
'Twas sad that he strayed from the ways of The Lord
'Tis a lesson for each one of us to learn
Never stray from God's heavenly ford

KING DAVID

After Saul's wrongdoing, Samuel mourned for him
Because The Lord repented He had made Saul king
But God spoke, *How long wilt thou mourn over Saul*
Pick thy self up now like a bird on the wing
Samuel did as The Lord had bade
As he knew it would gradually lead to joy
God then informed Samuel of another choice
'Twas to be a young shepherd boy

As a youth the boy toiled in open fields
And he lovingly tendered to his sheep
He enjoyed psaltery and loved to sing
With a voice so tender, sweet and deep
Goliath, a Philistine giant issued a challenge
To meet any Israelite warrior in combat
The fate of each nation depended on the outcome
Every Israelite was afraid like a frail trembling wombat

Though a youth, David faced a Philistine in battle
And Goliath was a giant of a man
But even though he was feared far and wide
David faced him with a sling and stone in hand

As Goliath charged forward with ferocious wrath
A stone from David's sling hit the giant's head
Goliath fell to his knees onto a stony path
And lay there in silence, still and dead
On hearing the outcome King Saul was delighted
And he proclaimed David a hero amongst his clan
But the friendship was not to last
As David became renowned as a great man

As he grew older, David was chosen to be king
And his fame became known throughout the land
Saul became jealous and sought to kill David
And he tracked him down over deserts of sand
Now Samuel did as The Lord had bade
And he anointed David to become king
Despite Saul's wrath and hatred against him
David responded not to a solitary thing

Much later after king Saul had died in battle
The men of Juda anointed David to the throne
He was to rule over them with wisdom
And became respected in every place and zone

King David ruled his kingdom with fairness
And through trials and betrayals he rose
He had many problems during his reign
But won many battles against his foes
During one of his many conquests
He did a very special thing
He brought The ark of the Covenant to Jerusalem
And the Israelites didst celebrate and sing

He was a good man and lived by the word of The Lord
However, he did commit a grave sin
He fell in love with Bethsabee who was Uria's wife
And Uria was a soldier of his own kin
He bade Bethsabee to come to his chamber
And he commanded her to sleep in his bed
He took advantage of her and she conceived
His immoral doing was of his own stead

He then ordered Uria to the front line of a battle
Knowing only too well he was likely to be slain
His evil deed came soon to the fore
And Uria died in agony and pain

Nathan, a prophet, approached David and reproached him
Why therefore hast thou despised God's law
Thou hast killed Urias with the blade of a sword
Thou deserves to be thrown way down below
As David broke down and confessed to The Lord
Nathem said, *God has taken away thy sin from thee*
Thou art forgiven and you wilt not die
But from woe and sadness thou shalt ne'er be free

When Bethsabee gave birth to the child
It was sickly and on the point of death
David ate nothing for seven days
But sadly the child cried and took its last breath
David strived hard and comforted his wife
And he went in unto her and they slept together
Bethsabee conceived and bore David a son
Who blossomed and grew like glorious heather

He was a bright boy and they named him Solomon
And he was to become the wisest man in the land
But in the meantime as he grew to manhood
King David ruled honestly with a touch of his hand

Later on in life, David wrote many songs and psalms
Which acted as a guidance to the whole of mankind
Despite his iniquity against his servant Urias
He remained faithful, true and one of a kind
So the moral about David's life
Despite his failings he was a man on whom one could depend
A poet. a shepherd and a king who ruled well
His legacy wilt live on until life's end

SOLOMON

In the latter days of King David' reign
The day drew nigh that he should die
He spoketh to Solomon, his son and heir
About the kingdom where his future lie
Solomon, I am going to the way of all flesh
Take courage my son and show thyself a man
Keep charge of The Lord thy God and all his ways
And rule thy people in the best way thou can

Pray for wisdom and do according to thy best
Strive always to achieve love and inner peace
Live by God's laws and he will be close to thee
He'll guide thee with a power of the golden-fleece
David passed away and slept with his fathers
Solomon sat on the throne and doted on his father's wish
His entire body filled with a pure sensation
He then knelt to his knees and prayed in heavenly bliss

And God appeared to Solomon in a dream
And he spoke, *Ask what thou wilt that I should give thee*
Solomon replied, *I am but a child and knowest not what to do*
And yet thou hast put all thy trust in me

Solomon then asked not for silver or gold
But for wisdom to judge his people throughout his reign
Give therefore to thy servant an understanding heart
Also wisdom to discern between good, evil and pain
God was pleased with his servant's request
And because he had not asked for riches and a long life
Nor had he sought the lives of his enemies
He blessed Solomon with a life free from strife

No other man shall be like thee throughout the world
For things thou didst not ask I give thee to wit
Riches and glory like no other king
Let it be so ... let it be writ
Then Solomon awoke he was wiser and more astute
He recalled everything about his dream
He called together all in his realm
And taught them how to be a reliable team

He became known far and wide
For all the wise Judgements he made
Hid realm prospered because of his wise ways
Solomon was grateful and every night he prayed

Two Women game before him to be judged
And between them they had just one child
They'd both given birth on the same day
But one of the babies perished and died
Both ladies swore that the child was hers
And no one knew exactly the truth
Each woman vowed she was the mother
But neither if them had sufficient proof

Solomon took heed of the women's words
He thought hard for a while and then he didst speak
Put the child down before me and bring me a sword
He then placed the blade 'gainst the baby's cheek
I wilt divide this living child into two
And I shall give half to one and half to the other
He raised the sword and was ready to strike
When he heard words from the baby's true mother

I beseech thee my lord, give to her the child alive
For I do now forever denounce my claim
The other woman said, Let it be neither yours nor mine
Divide the child and erase its name

Solomon took note of their requests and made his judgement
Give the child to this woman for it wilt not be killed
For surely she is the true mother of the child
And the true mother was so happy and thrilled
Solomon became known for being kind and just
And his kingdom grew across many countries wide
Kings came from afar to seek his advice
And by his counsel didst they abide

The queen of Saba heard of Solomon's fame
And she came to visit him with wealth untold
A great train of riches, precious stones and gold
She was met and welcomed into Solomon's fold
She proposed many things to King Solomon
And spoke of many things he already knew
She was taken aback by his wisdom and splendour
And showed him the respect that was due

She spoke, I heard of thy wisdom in mine own country

And I didst not believe what I had been told
Till I came here to see with mine own eyes
I now clearly see thy fame, wisdom and gold

And she gave King Solomon a precious gift
An abundance of rare spices and precious stones
One-hundred and twenty talents of gold
And silk to adorn his palace and domes
The queen returned home with her servants
But she came every year with a great measure
The weight was one-hundred and sixty-six talents of gold
Which added to King Solomon's eminent treasure

Hence, King Solomon exceeded all other kings in riches
His wisdom became known throughout the earth
Every kingdom desired to set eyes on his noble face
And each brought gifts to add to his worth
In the fourth year of his reign
He built a temple, a very sacred place
The outer walls of hewed mountain stone
The inner of cedar wood adorned in lace

On all the walls were diverse figures

Carvings of cherubim, 'midst tall palm trees
All the floor was overlaid with gold
And the temple exuded of a heavenly breeze

To honour The Lord, Solomon adorned the temple
He put an oracle in the midst of the place
In the inner he set there the ark
And there it remained in a state of grace
And the word of God came to Solomon
The Lord was pleased with what he had done
He displayed his pleasure in a special way
And blessed the temple 'neath a setting sun

Solomon was blessed in every way
But sadly he strayed from The Lord's heavenly path
He became besotted with many strange women
And he brought upon himself God's wrath
He loved women from Moab, Pherao and other lands
Edom, Siden and the Ethites he took for his wife
God Spoke, *Solomon, Do not go to these places*
Thou wilt adore false gods and change thy life

To these women he was besotted with a most ardent love

And he had seven-hundred wives as queens
He also had three-hundred concubines
All these women fulfilled his wanton dreams

And when he was old and grey
His heart turned away to false Gods
And as the women led him into wicked ways
He ceased to follow Gods guiding rods
He built shrines where his wives could worship
And their false gods he also adored
His wives burnt incense and offered sacrifices
All these things didst offend The Lord

God became angry with his sinful ways
He looked down on Solomon and said
I wilt divide and rend thy kingdom
And I shall give it to thy servant in stead
Nevertheless, in thy days I wilt not do it
Be it only for David, thy father's sake
But I will rend it out of the hand of your son
But his entire Kingdom I shalt not take

Neither will I takeaway the entire Kingdom

I wilt give one tribe to thy son
I do this for the sake of David my servant
And for all Israelites under the sun

Solomon ruled for forty years
The rest of his life was as written by the scribes
All his good works and words of wisdom
Benefited many countries, cities and tribes

JONAH

Jonah was a phophet and was the son of Amathi
And the Lord appeared to him in a dream one night
God said, *Arise and go to Ninive a great city*
For I wish them to repent and see the light
However, even though Jonah lived in God's ways
He was very illiberal and an obstinate man
God said, *I want thee to go Ninive*
And do for them all that thou can

The people therein hath committed grave sins
Lies, rape and sorcery are but of a few
I want thee to preach to the people
Warn them of the evil I am about to do
Just like the cities of Sodom and Gomorrah
If people did not repent and change their ways
God was about to rain fire down onto the land
He wouldst destroy their lives within forty days

But Jonah was very reluctant to do what God had asked
As for the people he had not an ounce of pity
He wanted nothing to do with the pagans
As he despised everything about Ninive City

So Jonah fled and went down to Joppe
From thence he headed for Tharsis aboard a ship
But he soon realised that he'd made a mistake
As he felt the wrath of The Lord's far reaching whip
The Lord sent a great wind o'er the water
And a great tempest was raised in the sea
All the mariners were afraid and cried out in fear
As there was no way to hide and flee

They were aware that Jonah was a Godly man
And they called upon him to kneel down and pray
Rise up and call thee upon thy God
Lest the boat sinks and we all perish this day
And each said to every one of his fellow men
Come, sit and let us speculate
Then we may know why this evil is upon us
And hence be saved from a terrible fate

And the lot fell upon Jonah
And they asked, *What caused this evil upon us*

Said Jonah, *I am a God fearing man*
And in The Lord I place my trust

They knew he had fled from the face of The Lord
And they asked, *Why hast thou dome this*
What shalt we do with thee
So the sea wilt calm into heavenly bliss
Jonah replied, *Take me and cast me overboard*
And the waters wilt be calmed for thee
It is what The Lord wants thee to do
The high wind wilt cease and calm the sea

And they took Jonah and cast him into the sea
The waters hushed and took on a moderate stage
And the men feared The Lord exceedingly
As the winds calmed and the sea ceased to rage
Now God had plans for Jonah
He prepared a great fish to swallow him whole
Jonah was in the belly for three days and nights
Awaiting the voice of God's heavenly call

When the time was right, God spoke to the fish
And it vomited Jonah onto dry land

And The Lord came to him a second time
So Jonah the prophet entered a land of sand

Now Ninive was indeed a pagan city
It was a site of depravity and sin
Jonah entered the city and began to preach
And their belief in God didst begin
The word came to the king of Ninive
And he rose up from his throne
He cast away his robe from him
And on his body only sackcloth was worn

All the people were aware of God's wrath
And the king didst make a decree
Let man nor beast take any food or drink
And all be dressed in sackcloth loose and free
Everyone repented and prayed to The Lord
Every thug, harlot, thief and wench
Each one was sorry for their iniquities
And The Lord endowed them with faith and strength

God wanted to teach Jonah a lesson
And He asked him, *Why art thou angry and forlorn*

Jonah knew he had offended The Lord
And replied, *It would be better had I not been born*

Then Jonah went out from the city
And he made himself a booth on which to sit
The Lord made ivy grow over his head
To give shade from the terrible heat to wit
Then God prepared a worm to devour the ivy
And the plant quickly suffered and died
The sun rose and there was a burning wind
Jonah broiled with the heat and openly cried

And God asked, *Hast thou reason to be angry*
Jonah replied *I am angry with reason even unto death*
God said *Thou art grieved for the ivy on which thou laboured not*
Thou shouldst pray for Ninive with thy last breath
Within the city are thousands of people
And they have all repented in The Lord's sight
Whereas before thou came to this place
They knew not their left hand from their right

Jonah realised his failings and sinfulness

And that only The Lord is allowed to Judge
He fell to his knees in repentance
And God didn't bear him a grudge

The moral is that God loves even the sinners
Which is a challenge to us all from above
God is all-seeing and everywhere
Jonah' tale displays the wideness of God's love

GOD CREATED LIFE ON EARTH

Constraints appear spectacularly fined tuned
For life to exist on earth as we know it
A good example is its distance from the sun
'Tis in a perfect position where it doth sit.
Its location is just right to keep temperature hospitable
'Tis relatively 120 degrees Fahrenheit and 40 degrees below
Further away from the sun we would freeze
If nearer we would bake, roast and glow

If anything altered even in a minute way
It would be impossible for life to exist at all
As necessary elements and molecules would not be produced
And these all play a most important significant role
Earth is an incomprehensible fine tuned machine
As David declared the wonders and glory of God
He spoketh of the cosmos and the firmament
Created by the power of The Lord's divine rod

The vast majority of the universe is unhabitable
'Tis to dense, too vacuous, too hot, too cold
Too dark, too bright and has too much radiation
No heavy elements for life to exist or unfold

Cosmos gravitational forces are far too intense
And the atmospheric environments are too unstable
Vast black holes, nebulae, asteroids and gases
Life couldn't exist in this unhealthy stable
Our position in the Milky Way is incredible
'Tis remarkable just how fortunate our cosmic location is
Exactly where it lies protects us form radiation
And dangerous star clusters, quavers and terrible bliss

Saturn, Jupiter, Uranus and Neptune are large planets
Each protect us from collision of asteroids fro' way out in space
If one got through and collided with earth
'Twould indeed be the end of the human race
Earth is charmed and not just for its location
It is 8000 miles in diameter and weighs trillions of tons
This is an ideal size and mass
And keeps us away from other dangerous suns

Less dense and its gravity could not retain atmosphere
Larger and denser ... there would be no air
Its atmosphere would be likened to Jupiter's
Not like earth where conditions are special and rare
Humans need many elements in order to survive
Oxygen, Carbon, hydrogen, potassium and so forth
Earth has just the tight amount of these
And helps to sustain life and keep it on course
Earth also has a rich abundance of heavy elements
That can be found sprinkled throughout its mantle and core
Mother Nature keeps them locked up and ready
To be released from her cosy store

Earth's distance from the sun and moon is perfect
They ensure a stable predictable orbit with a 24 hour day
Thus the planet doesn't get too hot or too cold
And the entire surface is warmed and cooled in a gentle sway
Thanks to our extraordinary large single moon
'Tis fifty times greater than any other moon-planet table
Earth is tilted at a nice gentle 23.5 degrees angle
And the moon keeps the earth's tilt gentle and stable

Planets that have small moons or no moon at all
Tend to have a rotational axis that tilts so badly

Without our moon, earth would experience catastrophic changes
And the tilt would waver and wobble e'er so sadly

As it is now we have predictable pleasant changes
And the earth can produce an annual supply of feed
We have seasons, spring, summer, autumn and winter
And each one is special ... so very special indeed.
The sun accounts for 99.9 per cent of our solar system
And one million earths could fit within it
We are grateful for its warmth and light
And for keeping our planet so bright and lit

The sun is a magnificent nuclear furnace
It warms us and we see clearly by its light
Plants absorb its energy and a magical process occurs
As the sun's position in the heavens is just right
If earth's gravity changed by just one per cent
Life on earth wouldn't exist at all
The precision of gravity is perfect
And takes on its heavenly call

Should any cosmic action change and fail
'Twould be impossible for life to exist at all
Did all these things come about by chance?

I think not ... 'twas by God's loving heavenly call

The material universe is subject to God's laws
The heaven's harmony is like a musical sound
The cosmos sings and relays a spiritual message
As the laws of the universe are Godly bound,

THE NEW TESTAMENT

THE GREATEST MAN WHO EVER LIVED

Can any man unquestionably be called the greatest man who ever lived?
How does one measure the greatness of a man
Is it by his physical strength or mental power
Or is it by his genius how he could think and plan
Or by the way he could make plants fruit and flower
No, a man's greatness is what he leaves behind him
What he leaves to grow and prosper mankind
Fresh lines to inspire and brighten the grim
Truth, integrity and kindness spring to mind

Of all the armies that marched the earth
And all the parliaments that ever sat and talked
None have ever left such a notable worth
As Jesus did throughout the life he walked
By His dynamic teaching and his way of life
Jesus raised people's hope and made their heart glow

He taught them how to love through life's trouble and strife
And truly affected their lives over two-thousand years ago

JESUS'S BIRTH AND FLIGHT
Jesus was born in Bethlehem in a stable bare
And was visited by three wise men from afar
They brought gold, frankincense and myrrh by fare
After travelling desert lands guided by a shining star
Angel Gabriel had visited Mary, an unmarried girl
To tell her she would conceive by the holy-spirit and give birth
This first of all threw the young girl into a whirl
For she would be despised by people throughout the earth

Mary asked angel Gabriel, *How can this be so*
For I am not having intercourse with a man?
She was informed that the holy spirit would flow
As it was all part of God's divine plan
Gabriel also gave Mary another message of hope
That her relative Elizabeth had also conceived a son
'Twas great news for Mary and helped her to cope

'Neath a deep blue sky and dazzling sun

Mary visits Elizabeth and receives a warm greeting
"Blessed art thou amongst women and blessed is your womb
I feel honoured by this celestial meeting
Thou hast blessed every corner of my house's room

When Elizabeth's boy was born she had to name her son
Protocol said he should be named after his dad
But she had been advised by Gabriel to
call the child John
And her husband Zechariah was happy and glad
The young boy was to become a holy sage.
And would baptise souls in the Jordon River
His sanctity showed even at an early age
And he displayed ways of a heavenly giver

When Mary returned home to her house
She was three months pregnant and didn't know
what to do
She was engaged to Joseph to be his spouse
And didn't know how to explain how she was due

Joseph was a good man and believed her reputation was pure
And he protected her because he loved her so
The penalty for unfaithfulness was stoning for sure
As it was an unforgivable sin in the name of the law

However, Joseph is troubled in spirit and mind
But in a dream an angel appeared to him
He convinced Joseph of how Mary was of a special kind
And how God had chosen her from out on a limb
When Joseph awoke he hearkened to what the angel had said.
He took Mary to his home as his wife
This public action served as a marriage ceremony in stead
And avoided lots of complications, worry and strife
Even though Mary is heavy with child they both depart
Joseph heads for Bethlehem the place of his birth
May be it was to meet new friends and make a new start
Whatever the reason, Joseph did it with all his worth

All the inns were full and for what it was worth
The only place available was a stable
In this dark dire place she gave birth
'Twas the beginning of a wonderful fable
She was visited by three foreign kings

And three shepherds also appeared on the scene
There was an atmosphere of angel's wings
A more holy place there ne'er has been

There wasn't a musical band in the room
And yet soft angelic music could be heard
Like flowers, the small stable started to bloom
And a sound hailed like the song of a bird

An angel tells them to have no fear
And it declares the good news and great joy
Suddenly, other angels didst appear
As in swaddling clothes lay a baby boy
Outside the fields were brightly lit by a shining star
It shone brightly over the keepers of sheep
It was the holiest of nights by far
An incredible feeling e'er so soft and deep

Time passed and when Jesus was forty days old
He was taken to the temple to be blessed
A tradition to be accepted into God's fold
Ordained by Moses's laws at God's request
Later an angel appears to Joseph and Mary
And tells them that they must pack up and flee
At first the couple are frightened and wary

But they have to abide in order to be free

King Herod had vowed to kill every boy child
And his orders were carried out by Roman soldiers cruel
Joseph and Mary flee on a donkey into the wild
To avoid the wicked fate of the king's rule

JESUS'S CHILDHOOD DAYS
Jesus grew up in Nazareth, a small town
A place where his brothers and sisters were born
He is the oldest of seven counting down
Blowing in the wind like ears of corn
Jesus also had cousins who lived miles away
Mary's sister Salome, has two young boys
There were John and James both happy and gay
Together they created lots of fun and noise

Joseph is a carpenter by trade
And as he raises Jesus as his own son
He teaches the boy how furniture is made
And stresses the importance of a job well done
The life of Joseph's family is built on God's laws
And they constantly had spiritual meetings
Joseph taught that a man shall reap whatever he sows

In order to receive heaven's angelic greetings

They pray every night before going to sleep
And every morning when they get out of bed
Their offerings were so sincere and deep
Their prayers were accepted by The Lord's good stead

Joseph took his family to the synagogue hall
To be taught all of God's spiritual ways
How to lead a good life towards a heavenly call
And to live with integrity all of their days
Every year they made a pilgrimage trip
To Jerusalem to celebrate the Passover
'Twas an act to be free from Satan's grip
And keep their souls in rays of clover

The annual trip usually took about two weeks
But when Jesus was twelve this didst change
As His countenance and thinking peaks
And His teaching now approached its celestial range
A problem came to light on the journey back home
Mary and Joseph presume that Jesus is with them
But then they realise he has started to roam
And find him amongst a group of theological men

At first when Jesus was nowhere to be found
They travel back to Jerusalem to look for him
But even there he is no where around
Things looked rather downcast and grim
Finally on the third day they go to the shrine
And there He is talking with the scribes
He was asking questions and feeling fine
And appeared to be picking up various vibes
However, Mary was upset and let Jesus know
Child, why did you treat us this way?
Jesus was surprised that they were troubled so
But apologised for causing any dismay

Why did you have to come looking for me?
Did you not realise I would be in this shrine?"
For I am destined to fulfil my father's decree
I assure you mother, every thing is fine
At that, Jesus returns home and is subject to their word
He grows in strength and in favour with God
From thence his countenance is like that of a bird
As he is blessed by God's divining rod

JESUS'S EARLY ADULT LIFE

Jesus was twenty-nine when he heard of John's fame
Who was preaching in towns around the Jordon River
John is indeed an impressive man in speech and name
And certainly stood out as a spiritual giver
His clothing was basic made up of camel hair
With a leather girdle around his loins and back
The rest of his body was bronzed and bare
But his words and deeds were on a heavenly track

John cared not for gold or money
His thoughts were for the souls of mankind
His food was locusts and wild honey
Baptism in the Jordon was his daily grind
His message excited every single woman and man
Many realised their need to kneel and repent
They made their way forward like a new born fan
And he baptised each one as time was spent

Alas, some Pharisees and Sadducees approached him
But John condemns them and sent them away

"You off-springs of vipers living a life so grim
Thou must change thy evil ways this very day

Produce fruit that befits the laws of God
And do not presume you are good men
The axe lies at your feet where thou hast trod
Thy fate wilt be scored by the stroke of a pen

Many ask John if he is a prophet or a holy one
He replies he is but a simple man of the earth
Many like him have already passed and gone
And many should have listened with all their worth
Some Levites asked if he had the right to baptise
And if he was Elijah or another holy gent
I baptise in water, John simply replies
'Tis a way for souls to kneel and repent

Later, Jesus visits the Jordon and approaches John
And he asks John to baptise Him
John feels touched under a burning sun
And began to dither in every nerve and limb
*But my cousin, I am the one who needs baptising by thee
For even when I was in my mother's belly
My heart beat jumped with gladness and glee*

And my entire body quivered like a wobbly jelly

Jesus's baptism was a symbol from above
Immediately after coming up from the stream
The spirit of a dove appeared to Him above
'Twas likened to an angelic heavenly dream
Something spiritual happened during the holy act of love
Jesus recalls all his celestial life in heaven
And a voice resounds from the sky above
This is my son, my beloved breathren

After His baptism, Jesus has a lot to think about
As heaven has opened to discern many Godly things
And now He is driven into the wilderness
And tested by marvels that temptation brings
Immediately afterwards the spirit drove Jesus forth
Into a desert where he was to spend forty days and forty nights
Indeed He was approached by the devil on course
And tempted high within high mountainous sights

If thou art the son of God turn these stones into bread
But Jesus performs not for His own desire

But only for The Lord's ways and good stead
A guideline to avoid the flames of hellfire

If thou art the Son of God, throw thyself down from here
God wilt keep thee safe within His stead
His angels wilt protect thee e'er so pure and dear
And naught shall harm a single hair on thy head

It is written The Lord God wilt thou worship
And only Him wilt thou serve
Keep always aboard the Almighty's ship
Lest thou should slide down a slippery curve

Jesus was hungry and Satan tempted him many times
All the kingdoms of the world I wilt give thee
Just to abide by my ways and signs
But Jesus stuck to God's law and away the devil did flee

JESUS PREACHES TO THE PEOPLE

Jesus left the misery of the cold mountain air
And was ready to commence his true vocation in life
To minister and preach to all sundry and fair
And to teach how to cope with misery and strife
Peter and Andrew were the first two of Jesus' clan
And the next two disciples were John and James
He asked them to become fishes of man
And promised to guide them down spiritual lanes

As Jesus preached to many people and tribes
Quoting many parables inspiring and swell
He troubled and incited high priests and scribes
Who were entrapped in the pit falls of hell
Do all that the high priests say and teach
But do nothing of their acts and deeds
Their teaching is true within the Lord's reach
Alas, their actions are likened to badly sown seeds

As Jesus spoke truly from a pure heart
The scribes knew what he taught was true
And that God's laws and theirs were so far apart
Therefore, they schemed to kill Him through and through

Jesus made His way to Galilee close to His home
As He and his family were invited to a wedding fine
Alas, some of the guests started to moan
The hosts had almost run out of special put-by wine
Mary approaches the ministers in charge of ways
And advises them to do whatever Jesus may seek
Well, there were six large stone jars in the bays
Jesus says, *Fill each with water to its peak*
-

The ministers then served the happy guests
And everyone became joyful and gay
As it was wine at its ultimate best
And it brightened up the couple's special day

This was the first miracle of Jesus' reign
It was just one of many more yet to come
Blind and lame people and souls in pain
Mentally afflicted along with the deaf and the dumb
Jesus went and preached to everyone around
And they brought to Him many people who were sick
On touching them they were immediately cured and sound
And their eyes shone like a lit candle wick

The vast crowds of people were too many to count
But they all listened eagerly to what Jesus had to say
As He related the famous Sermon on the Mount
And taught them the meaning of God's way

FEEDING OF THE FIVE-THOUSAND

Great crowds followed Jesus from a distance far away
To perhaps see a miracle and to hear him talk
But they were all tired and hungry by the third day
And most were exhausted and could barely walk
Jesus advised His disciples to feed the crowd
But all they had were five loaves and two fish
They gave the food to Jesus and He prayed and bowed
To feed the five-thousand was his solemn wish

Jesus ordered the crowd to recline on the ground
And He asked His disciples to dish out the food
They realised there was plenty to go all around
And the multitude ate happily in a sombre mood
Each person was happy by what they ate
And fragments gathered were twelve baskets full
The great crowd sat quietly and could hardly wait
For Jesus to resume with His blessed call

As the crowd started to return to their home
Jesus asked His disciples to get into a boat
He then went to pray in a quiet zone
And there He meditated to gather His thought

When Jesus finished He was all alone
But the disciples' boat was in a buffeted sea
He made his way to the perilous zone
And could hear the sound of an anguished plea
Jesus walked on the water buffeted by fierce waves
On seeing Him, the apostles cried out in fear
But Jesus says, *Do not to be afraid*
Thou art safe whilst I am here

But Peter answered, *My Lord if it is thou*
Bid me to come over the water to thee
Jesus replied, *Come to me as thou dost know how*
But Peter was afraid and sank in the raging sea
Lord save me! Peter cried out in a terrified state
Jesus stretched out and took hold of his hand
Peter's lack of faith was his ruling fate.
A little later they were safe on dry land

MORE MIRACLES

About this time Jesus hears of John the Baptist's death
King Herod's wife Herodias hated John so
She desired to see him take his last breath
His head on a plate made her eyes glow
Jesus returns to Galilee the place of His home
And here another miracle takes place
A high government official of Kings Herod's throne
Approached Jesus with apparent misery on his face

The official approaches Jesus with an anguished cry
And tells him his son is critically ill indeed
He implores Jesus not to let his son die
And Jesus replied with a typical creed
On his way back to his domain
The officer is met by his servants true
They tell him his boy is well and free from pain
And his countenance is bright like the morning dew

Jesus moves on to the Sea of Galilee
And there he locates four disciples more
His disciples are fishing by the sea
And He tells them to cast their net to the sea floor

Peter replies they have caught nothing during the entire night
But he does as Jesus had said
Another miracle happens within each apostle's sight
Such a great multitude of fish in their stead

Whilst preaching in an old discarded inn
A paralysed man was lowered from the roof in a cot
Jesus wasn't offended by the boisterous din
And He cured the man there and then on the dot
Jesus performed many more miracles in his stead
And his fame spread throughout the land
He even raised Lazarus from the dead
His followers became like grains of sand

Jesus came across some Pharisees and scribes
And they were about to stone a woman to death
She was guilty of adultery with lots of men
And now in danger of taking her last breath
Master they said with anger in their eyes
This woman is guilty of adultery, a terrible crime
She has broken Moses' law under God's skies
It is written she must die under pelts of stone and lime

Jesus pondered for just a little while
For it was an act for which she had to atone
He walked close to the scribes with a gentle smile
Let the one amongst thee without sin cast the first stone
Hearing this, one by one they didst turn and flee
Turning to the lady, Jesus spoke and said,
Woman, where are they ... no one has condemned thee
Go away now and sin no more in thy stead

One miracle took place on the Sabbath day
And it concerned a man with a withered hand
High priests and scribes watched closely at bay
To see Jesus perform something fine and grand
The high priests were impressed by Jesus' deed
But they were there for another reason
The accused Jesus of defiling a holy creed
As though He'd committed an act of treason

They said it was unlawful to perform on the Sabbath day
But Jesus quoted a riddle with a clout
Which one amongst you would stand by and stay
If one of thy sheep fell into a pit and couldn't get out?

They stood there in silence knowing not what to say
So Jesus asks the man to stretch his hand out
The man's hand is cured making him happy and gay
The scribes are furious without any doubt

Jesus continues with His good works and deeds
He cures the blind, lepers and lots who are ill
People are impressed by his miraculous creeds
And by His manner to fulfil God's holy will

In a great multitude, Jesus is crushed by many a soul
And yet he senses a lady's gentle prod
He felt stability leave His body for a heavenly call
The lady's faith healed her via God's divining rod
She had been suffering from a bad blood flow
And immediately was healed and felt fine.
A smile appeared on her face and her eyes didst glow
Her whole countenance displayed a miraculous sign

THE CRUCIFIXION

The Pharisees and high priests detested all Jesus' work
As he brought all their evil doings to the fore
They followed Him around to listen and lurk
And wished Him to come crashing to the floor
Jesus spoke about the Pharisees and their ways
And advised people to obey their commands
But not to act according to their acts and praise
For they talk but do nothing on remand

Woe to you hypocritical scribes and Pharisees
For you do not treat your brethren fair
You should fall down onto bended knees
The way thou treats all souls in thy care

The Pharisees and high priest became filled with hate
And they planned to have Jesus slain
His preaching denounced all their laws and state
And exposed their devious ways of pain and gain
And it came to pass when Jesus' work was near its end
He informed His apostles He was about to die
And ate a last supper with them at a special trend
And explained to them the very reason why

He took bread, then blessed and broke it
He gave it to His disciples and said
Take it and eat this tiny bit
This is my body in good stead
He did the same with a cup of wine
Which in grace was Jesus' blood
And represented the fruit of the vine
And everything on earth that is just and good

Then Jesus' took His disciples to a secluded park
And there for hours he fervently prayed
He was then arrested by soldiers in the dark
And marched off by official orders bade
Despite all his good works, Jesus was betrayed
The Pharisees despised Him and bore Him a grudge
They plotted and connived an evil charade
And then handed Him over to Pilate, a Roman judge

Pilate sensed Jesus' innocence and wished Him to be freed
But the high priests incited and roused the angry crowd
He was condemned by corrupt Pharisee creed
Crucify Him ... crucify him! the angry mob cried out loud

Now Pilate, seeing he was doing no good
Washed his hands and delivered Jesus over to Roman stead
And Jesus was severely scourged by orders rud
And a crown of thorns placed upon His head
After mocking Him they removed His clothes
To be crucified they handed Him a cross
Jesus appeared weary like a wilted rose
As soldiers taunted Him in a manner e'er so gross

Jesus was then nailed to the cross by his hands and feet
Soldiers then divided His clothes casting bids
And appeared proud of their gruesome feat
One even jabbed a spear into Jesus' ribs
Even on the cross despite severe suffering and pain
Jesus' thoughts were pure like the early morning dew
He turned His eyes towards heaven in thunderous rain
Father forgive them for they know not what they do

Alongside Jesus, two robbers were also hung thus
And one of them turned to Jesus and said
If thou art the Christ, save thyself and us
Save us from being slain and dead

But the other robber rebuked him in his stead
Dost not even thee fear God even at the end of life
We are both guilty of the charges read
But this man is completely innocent of any trouble and strife
He then turned to Jesus his bloodstained head
Lord, remember me in thy kingdom up in the skies
Jesus turned to the thief and quietly said
Amen, today thy shalt be with me in Paradise

When Jesus died, darkness overshadowed the land
And it lasted for nine hours or more
The earth moved and scattered stones in the sand
Large rocks were rent and shook to their core
Jesus encouraged us to love and care for each other
His message was of compassion and love
To love our enemies as a sister or brother
And strive to share like the heavens above

For this very reason Jesus had come down to earth
He had died and took on the sins of mankind
It was His destiny before the day of His birth
A more greater man never e'er wilt thou find

POEMS BY BARRY

The following 5 wonderful poems were
composed by my younger brother, Barry.
I feel so honoured to present them alongside my own
work.

DEUS DIVES MISERICORDIA (God is rich in mercy.)

Thank you little humble bumble bee,
For the thoughts that came to me.
As in church I saw you lay,
On that cold mid-winter's day.
Poor dying, little humble bumble bee,
Why should you have such thanks from me?
'Twas by pure chance I saw you lay,
On the church's aisle that wintry day.

Did you venture out too soon,
Thinking February was June?
Methinks ... perhaps you could not wait,
So many flowers to pollinate.
Poor dying, little humble bumble bee ... so keen,
How sorely tried you must have been.
To see the trees of blossoms bare,

To feel the cruel mid winter's air.
The church's door was opened wide,
And ... having found yourself inside.
Cold, hungry ... and in disarray,
Exhausted on the church aisle you lay.
The creature before the Creater lay,
On that cold February day.
'Twas there we met ... perhaps by chance,
But somehow ... I feel providence.

For now ... to you I must convey,
That when I first knelt down to pray.
Although I tried ... hard as can be,
No form of prayer would come to me.
I felt so sorry for you there,
'Twas then my thoughts turned into prayer.
And because of a little humble bumble bee,
'God's Dazzling Mercy' came to me.

My Lord! If a spark of pity can come from me,
For a little humble bumble bee.
How much more ... beyond all imagination,
Is the love of God for all his creation.

And I thought upon Jesus' Holy Name,
Formed in a dazzling burning flame.
My risen saviour from Heaven above,
Ah! So many countless sparks of love.
Ah! Little bee ... let me explain,
Your brief stay here was not in vain.
Oh no! Your mission in this life was love,
To lift my eyes to my God above.

And it surely was your blessed fate,
No earthly flowers to pollinate.
You did not fail! You reached your goal,
Your pollen touched my very soul.
So thank you little humble bumble bee,
For the hope you brought to me.
I'm glad we met. Ah no ... 'twas not by chance,
But by Good God's Loving Providence.

Deo Gratias.
Barry Cowell.

THE LITTLE SPARK.

Have you ever marvelled at
The brightness of the sun?
So dazzling ... with a radiance
We scarce can look upon

And have you ever pondered
As it shines o'er land and sea,
That nothing in this whole wide world
Could ever brighter be?

Ah! But there's a brighter radiance
Yes! Even brighter than the sun!
And it can be found ... if we'll but look
In each and everyone.

It is the little spark of good
In every soul we meet.
On the highway of this life
On each and every street.

Look always for this spark of good
E'en when the heart seems bare.
And always – always you will find
Some little flicker there.

For it is a reflection
Of God's love for you and me.
No countless dazzling suns
Could ever brighter be.

For whenever clouds assail you
Look for the little spark.
For the dazzling hope of the risen lord,
Shines fiercely through all dark.

One day this veil will vanish
And, in God's own time you'll be.
With your saviour ... light of the world
For all eternity.

Barry Cowell.

PLEASE HELP ME FIND THE KEY.

Oh dear and loving Jesus
Please take me to Your heart.
I feel – oh insecure
When we are apart.

I know I'm just not worthy
To even speak Your name.
And yet for me, You gladly died
When down to earth You came.

You came so meek and humble
Born in a stable poor.
No worldly riches to Your name
Just swaddling clothes You wore.

Nailed to the cross of Calvary
The soldiers mocked You so,
And yet You loved them crying loud
"Forgive – they do not know!"

And still Your love was flawless
As turning to the thief.
Your promise was eternal life
Because of his belief.

How much You must have suffered
Your sorrow now complete.
To see Your mother Mary
Stood weeping at Your feet.

And how it must have severed
Your Mother's heart to see.
Her bleeding dying Jesus
Pure lamb of Calvary.

Remind me then my Jesus
If from Your path I stray.
Remind me of Your mother's heart
As in her arms you lay.

Christ Jesus make me hearken
Please help me find the key.
Most sacred heart of the loving Christ
I place my trust in thee.

My one true saviour
I place my hope in thee.

Barry Cowell.

LOVE IS THE KEY

God of love- my father
And my unchanging friend.
I long so much to meet You
At my life journey's end.

I know You won't refuse me
When I ask in Jesus' holy name.
To lift my eyes to Heaven
In bright sunshine or in rain.

Holy spirit in my exile
Lift my eyes to Heaven above.
Whisper to me of God's glory
Of my saviour's burning love.

Shepherd of love – beyond compare,
Take to Thy heart my pilgrim prayer.
'Look upon my eyes, that I will always see
That Christ Jesus is love
And love is the key.

Barry Cowell.

THE WIDOW'S MITE

Brother sister pilgrims – in Jesus' holy name
As you travel on life's way.
This little verse is sent to you
A message to convey.

To remind you of Christ's parable
Of the widow's mite.
How so infinitely precious
The small coin was in God's sight.

Your heart united to Christ's loving heart,
Is the widow's mite.
To help your brother-sister pilgrims
To their Heavenly home of light.

For, when in Jesus' holy name
You ask the lord above.
He will make your heart - the widow's mite
A channel of God's love.

Barry Cowell

POEMS FOR LEADING A GOOD LIFE

All the following poems are not exactly biblical but in my mind they are spiritual and a guidance to help us lead a good life.

I never classed myself as a poet but I feel I was inspired spiritually to put these words into verse. I sincerely hope you like them.

INTEGRITY

Integrity is the practice of being honest
With morals truthful and good
Ethical principals are uncompromising
Living the good life as all of us should

A person of integrity can be trusted
Even as deep secrets tend to unfold
Qualities shine from him like starlight
With morals far more precious than silver and gold

Just as a flower blossoms in springtime
And gives off a beautiful perfume like hue
Our span of life on earth is brief
And yet long enough to be honest and true

LIVE BY THE LAWS OF GOD
IN THE BEGINNING WAS THE WORD
AND THE WORD WAS WITH GOD
AND THE WORD WAS GOD

The moon, the stars and all that we are seeing
Everything that exists emanated from a supernatural being
God stretched out his hand and the earth hangeth on nothing
To understand God's heavenly works is intensively crushing

Think not to gain any ill gotten feat
Lest thou are filled with guile and deceit
Our lifetime is the passing of a shadow or shroud
'Twill pass away like the trace of a cloud

Love nature and respond to it hither and thither
Clothe thyself in purity and respond e're it tends to wither
Let us not be in need of meadow or lea
Soak it up like the beauty of the deep blue sea

So as to keep our lives true, nice and bright
Cast away darkness, put on an armour of light
Strive to lead a good life and create a spark
For evil doers love to reside in the dark

They feel light will expose their evil deeds
In the dark they canst plant their wicked seeds
Live well and become stable as an old oak tree
Draw close to The Lord and he will be close to thee

Live a good life and feel open and free
Resist the devil and he will flee from thee
A lamp of the wicked deepens, flickers and fades
Whereas the lamp of integrity flows like the everglades

Be kind to thy neighbour, be true to thy word
Be a friend to the world and be in enmity with The Lord

We all have faults and we should be aware of that.

FAULTS

Life is full of trials and tribulations
And we are of't put to the test
Striving relentlessly to reach our goal
To give our loved ones nought but the best

But then ... none of us are perfect
We all have faults and flaws
Unlike the one who fell into a cesspit
And came out smelling like a rose

Always strive to keep an open mind
Or into a pit thou could fall
And avoid the greatest of faults
Which is ... to be conscious of none at all

KNOWLEDGE

Liken knowledge to a garden

Cultivate it like a just cause

And when it's time to be harvested

It will come to prominence like a rose

IMAGINATION

Imagine the close of a hot summer's day
Stars a twinkling and the moon starts to loom
Atmosphere vibrantly fresh and clean
The sweet attar of a crimson rose in bloom

Imagine a majestic oak tree tall and strong
From a tiny acorn ... it has surpassed its test
Home to countless creatures sheltered by its leafy bough
How many tiny chicks have flown the nest?

Imagine lily white clouds in the heavens
A gleaming raindrop stirred by a soft breeze
The shimmering beauty of multiple colours
A red admiral fluttering 'tween verdant trees

Imagine a soft breath of wind
As it stirs corn and pastures new
And a reflected moon quivers and trembles
Upon a rippling pond in waters blue

Imagine a garden adorned with flowers
And how many seeds still remain inside
Awaiting their short span of life on earth
To exhibit exquisite beauty ... bursting with pride

Imagine birds singing in harmonic ease
Watching bees flitting from rose to rose
An abundance of perpetual peace
A state of calm and sweet repose

Imagine all these beautiful things
A garden of Eden yet to be
'Tis a bounty well within our grasps
If only we would, but open our eyes ... and see!

THE NIGHT SKY

To gaze upon a clear night sky
As another day approaches its end
'Tis a tiny glimpse of heaven
As each star dost twinkle and blend

Stars are so very far away
Yet so pleasing to my sight
Nebulas, moons and distant suns
A truly majestic gift of the night

The moon rises over a landscape
'Neath a star laden bright sky
Highlighting the beauty of Nature
Wonderful vistas far and nigh

As I gaze in wonder at fleeting clouds
Tears of emotion well up in my eyes
'Tis a privilege to behold God's creation
A tiny glimpse of Paradise

GOD'S GLORY

The heavens declare God's glory
'Tis a true and wonderful story
The firmament proclaimed his handi-work
Where nebulae and shining stars doth lurk

The word of The Lord refreshes the soul
And keeps mind bright, healthy and whole
Ne'er a word or a prayer is not heard
'Tis received in heaven like the song of a bird

God's commands are enlightening to the eye
They are highly recommended to you and I
Fear of The Lord is pure and endures forever
And lightens the heart like a breath of heather

Live a life of purity as thy life doth unfold
'Tis a special gift far more precious than gold
Speak favourable words as thy mouth doth speak
Kind words tend to uplift the mild and the meek

From wanton sin, strive to restrain
'Twill only end up in sorrow and pain
Feeling downcast and sorrowful ... The Lord will address
And He'll always comfort you in times of distress

Whilst walking in an American desert I came across a large rock adorned by the most beautiful flowers.

A LONELY ROCK

A rock lay bare in a desert
Surrounded by driftwood and sand
The rock was lonely, yet happy
Because of past happy times in the land
It had once been surrounded by flowers
Blowing in the wind with a quaint, elegant flair
An oasis of beauty and tranquillity
That flourished in the cool night air
The stone and the flowers united
As one ... they became part of the scene
Alluring, graceful ... exquisite
A more beautiful site ne'er has been
The reason why the rock is now lonely
Is 'cos the flowers wilted and withered away
All the stone has now are memories
Times of beauty, swagger and sway
Now in its loneliness ... the rock clearly recalls
Sheer happiness 'mongst the flowers
It feels better for having lived with beauty
Be it only for a few special hours
The moral behind the little rock's tale
Is to absorb natural beauty, all around
Because beauty is uplifting and refreshing
Like all nature's gifts from the ground

UNFAVOURABLE WAYS OF MEN

Time on Earth is fleeting

And a man's life is a gift sublime

When he comes to meet his maker

He will be judged by his footprints in time

Beware ye men of wanton destruction

Lest thy ways of avarice yet untold

Be brought to the forefront of justice

And your life of greed and malice start to unfold

Liken thy mind to an ascetic fakir

Rid thyself of false worldly goods thine

Scorn not underprivileged below thee

Lest thou are lost in the sea of brimstone and brine

GOD'S CREATION.

Have you ever marvelled at Nature
So many picturesque scenes of intricate design
Snow-capped mountains, lakes and crannies
Countless artistic sculptures exquisitely divine.
Lily white clouds floating gracefully in the sky
The moon, the stars ... and our life giving sun
Each one created by the One most high
Many more our eyes have yet to feast upon

Each dawn the sun starts to rise
Displaying majestic scenes in its wakes
A blue sky and meandering clouds
Are mirrored in awesome natural lakes
Did all this beauty come about by chance
Or was it created by a divine celestial being?
It can only be as written in Genesis
These wonderful things we are seing

A LIFETIME

Love justice and feel integrity of the heart
Perverse counsels separate a man from The Lord
A good man seeks out justice to impart
An evil man promises but never keeps his word

A poor man who lives with integrity
Is far richer than a wealthy evil man
A rich man wilt rend a man to bended knee
A poor man will help his neighbour whenever he can

Our lifetime is the passing of a shadow
And wilt pass away like the traces of a cloud
It will disperse like a floating mist
And disappear within a far-reaching crowd

Life is short and cannot be deferred
It is fixed with a seal, no one ever comes back
So, be wise and keep God's commandments
Be prudent and honest, and keep thyself on track

In time, even our name will be forgotten
And no-one will remember our deeds
No one ever comes back from the nether world
'Tis now time to plant heavenly seeds

However, all souls are in the hand of God
Fear The Lord and thou can rest in peace
Be kind to the downcast, the poor and the needy
And thou shalt be welcomed like a golden fleece

Strive to live with wisdom and integrity
For the fruit of a noble man is glory
Unfailing is the root of understanding
Wisdom will turn thy life into a wonderful story

There is joy when a child first lifts his hands
Yet all too soon comes the final end
Therefore seek out wisdom from a special band
And heaven awaits thee around the bend

Put thy trust in The Lord and understand truth
Be faithful and abide with Him in love
Because truth, grace and purity are His chosen ones
They shall reside with the angels in the heavens above

SEEK OUT WISDOM

To be a wise person, honest and true
Prepare thy words and thou shalt be listened to
A man to be trusted is he who keeps his word
A prudent man puts his trust in the ways of The Lord
Live a life of integrity, be honest and true
Whilst breathe is in you, let no man dominate you
Lead a good life and create a beautiful story
Keep control over your affairs, let no one tarnish thy glory
Exalt not too much a rich man or a celebrity
Perfect wisdom is found in a man of integrity.
Guard well thy tongue lest from it evil drips
The venom of an asp derives from its lips
Do goodness throughout thy life and smile
A true soul is where there is no evil nor guile
The wind's sound can be heard as it blows
Yet fro' where it comes from no one knows
Never cause trouble or friction in thy neighbours wake
Lest thou cause tears to fall from a lachrymal lake
When deciding what is wrong or what is true
A man's conscience will keep his soul on cue.

WORDS OF WISDOM

A man wise for himself alone has full enjoyment and all around him praise his endeavour

A man wise for his neighbour wins glory and his name endures forever

When man is wise to his own advantage his fruits are to himself alone

When a man is wise for his neighbour his fruits are enduring and never 'e'er forlorn

A false friend will share your joys but in times of trouble he stands afar

A true friend bears with you in times of joy and sadness and leaves his door ajar

.

Use the tongue wisely and keep the truth intact
A word is the source of every deed, thought or act
Guard well thy tongue lest from it evil drips
The venom of an asp derives from its lips
The tongue can be a mistress of death and life
Speak always the truth like a dutiful wife
Use the tongue wisely as its branches shoot forth
Words of wrath and lies steers a life off course

I LIKE

I like the sound of a babbling brook

The buzzing of a fragile dragonfly

I like every creature in the sea

Every bird that adorns the sky

I like tulips and daffodils that bloom in early Spring

The dawn chorus as early birds begin to sing

I like snow-capped mountains and sky e'er so blue

The crispness of a new day ... early morning dew

I like soothing music and how a skylark sings

It touches my soul like a canzonet on angel's wings

I like Arcadian lifestyle ... especially first season of the year

Yong lambs appear in leas ... a sight so very dear

I like nature in its entirety ... each season

with its special trend

God willing, I'll always love and cherish Nature 'til life's end.

This poem is about what can happen when man doesn't live by God's laws. His evil ways cause sorrow and devastation to people within his wake
I was born just prior to the outbreak of World War Two. Lots of orphanage children were shipped off to Australia with the promise of a good life. However, this wasn't to be as many rich businessmen profited on their misery.

POOR LITTLE ORPHANS

Fear amongst the orphans
As rumors spread around
Lots of tiny infants
Listed ... Australia bound
Pure greed 'mongst the gentry
'Twas the ministers' intent
In order to line their pockets
Shanghai poor little English gents

Poor mites with meagre belongings
Scaled gangway filled with glee
Not realising .... sailing seaward
Ne'er again to see family
A six week's long journey
Comforting each other ... a merry little band

But soon their dreams were shattered
On reaching a foreign land

Gathered and herded together
'Neath a blazing sun up high
Trudged o'er hazardous landscape
Throats all parched and dry
Crowded into a dismal attic room
Unhappy and frightened in their plight
Poor little blighters huddled together
To help them get through the night

Early morning brought task masters
Overloading with arduous work
Scrubbing and other laborious tasks
Ne'er a chance to rest or shirk
Back breaking work in fields
With shovel, pick and spade
Furrowing bake hardened ground
Planting whatever they were bade

The plight of poor forgotten souls
'Stead of being tucked up in a cosy bed
Condemned to a life of drudgery
Was all that lay ahead

A shame on British ministers
Sentencing little innocents to a life of strife
Profiteering on the backs of babes
So as to live a wealthier life
Youngters 'tween the age of six and ten
Had to strive in sunshine, rain or frost
Stolen from them ... a precious gift
Their childhood ... 'twas up and lost

My wife Elsina, was on holiday in France and she came across an old lady beggar and was taken aback by what she saw. She was so touched by the event that she asked if I would write a poem about it.

THE OLD LADY BEGGAR AND THE ROSE
On the corner of't street sat a little old lady
Her skin all wrinkled, wi' bags under her eyes
She'd sit there for hours on end
Beggin' wi' an old oxo tin 'tween her thighs
Poor old Peggy wer' just part o' scene
She'd done it for thirty years or more
Most people just walked by as if she weren't there
But an odd one would throw coppers on't floor
She'd pick up an old penny wi' her bent fingers
An hold it in't middle of her palm
It oft' took her back to her youth
When she'd beauty, elegance and charm
But one day, something special happened
As she sat there in a typical pose
A gentleman placed not a penny in her hand
But instead, the most beautiful, colourful rose

It touched old Peggy so much
To realise that someone did really care
Especially coming from a stranger
And one with elegance and flair
A deep feeling stirred deep inside her
A beautiful sensation ran down her arm
It encompassed all of her being
Making her body feel tingly and warm
In Peggy's oncoming years
Especially in times of duress and strife
The kindness shown by a stranger
Remained within her the rest of her life

MAKE THE RIGHT CHOICE

In life we arrive at a junction
And there are two paths to choose
One is filled with gold and riches
The second appears full of the blues
If you wish to fly on a cloud to heaven
'Tis now a choice you must make
To choose the golden path 'stead of the stony
'Tis an unwise option ... a dreadful mistake
To choose the hard path is difficult
But 'tis the only moral thing to do
It may ardous and stony
But is pure like a flower's hue
Always strive to be true to thyself
And in times of trouble and strife
The Lord will always stay by thy side
'Til the end of thy foreseeable life
As dawn breaks, make a vow to be good
And to help thy fellow man on his way
If by nightfall you are at peace with yourself
Then is has been a successful day

BE WISE

Don' linger on things so very wrong
Be of men that are so few
Keep integrity where it doth belong
Make sure always your words ring true

Your word is your bond ... 'tis like a band of gold
Speech derives from your very soul
Harness it, caress it ... 'tis a thing to behold
And your life will enhance ten fold
Strive to avoid acts of gossip and slander
Strive always to do your best
Let your deeds be of honesty and candour
Be moral and virtuous ... the ultimate test
Harken then to words of wisdom
Nor cause anyone grief or strife
Never e'er speak words of venom
'Twill lead to a happier life
Put all evil thoughts to one side
Cast away false riches come about by ill begot
Lest from the devil thou hast to hide
For the sun will rise and shine when you are not

Strive to never e'er commit deeds of wrath
Solomon was a ruler ... a very wise king
But even he strayed from the good path
'Tis hard ... as wisdom is a God given thing

CUSTODIANS

If animals disappear there won't be any more to take their place
And a slice of God's earth will be missed
We should take care of their habitats with an air of grace
And look after them with love and heavenly bliss
We are custodians of this planet and all that's on it
And if we don't care then nobody will
I've watched many animals survive by sheer courage and wit
To keep them on track 'twould my heart fulfil
Animals in their habitat can touch a man's soul
They live by the laws of nature in part
Doing so they reach The Lord's heavenly call
And touch the very eccles of my heart
As I look up to my maker I am struck dumb
I am taken aback in awe and reverence
To help animals sustain a natural rule of thumb
'Twould surely make a vast blessed difference

WISDOM

Solomon sought wisdom even as a child
To man she is an unfailing pleasure
She e'er so faithful, so meek and mild,
And wilt forever un-lease God's treasure
She's a teacher and prophet of God's way
If a man wishes for riches in his life
Nothing is more useful or likely to pay
Wisdom is likened to a faithful wife

She knows in advance the outcome of ages
The beginning, the mid-point and the end of times
Let wisdom into thy heart like the biblical sages
Liken thy soul to blessed mystical chimes
Learn about years and the position of stars
About the temper and nature of wild beasts
The power of the wind and elements afar
Why a sheep is so designedly fleeced

Wisdom is an aura in the sight of the Lord
She's an effusion that display's God's glory
One of her standards is the impeccable word
Take her into your heart ... create a magical story

God is close to one in whom wisdom doth dwell
For from them doth radiate truth, integrity and light
The preaching of wisdom rings a hallowed bell
Soul and body shines e'er so clear and bright
A man of wisdom is unsullied and clean
And he abides and adheres to God's laws
To keep's God's commandments e'er so keen
And the angels in heaven sing his applause

A wise man is enamoured by her beauty
And he taketh her forth to be his bride
She's an instructress of all God's work and duty
Is loyal and will work by his side
If riches be a desirable possession in life
Wisdom is far richer above all other things
For who is more prudent through trouble and strife
She has lifted and empowered many reigning kings

Justice, fortitude and love she preaches
She is refulgence of eternal light
Follow the example of all that she teaches
And yours will be a world heavenly bright

She knows things of old and things yet to come
She keeps the commandments throughout the ages
She understands riddles and wonders of God's kingdom
As described by the bible's prophets and sages
She is fair and brighter than the sun's essence
And surpasses even a constellation of stars
Compared to light she takes precedence
And brightens up all the heavens afar

Wisdom is mobile beyond all earth's motions
She penetrates and pervades by purity
Fills a soul with spiritual lotions
And creates a resilient celestial unity
God peers from above onto an ordinary man
And can see all his troubles and woes
A soul strives hard for family and clan
But knoweth what he reaps he dost sow

God's message is the keep the devil at bay
To seek wisdom throughout trouble and strife
Attempt to acquire wisdom during each day
'Twill lead to a much happier life

STRIVE

Strive to be better ... strive to atone
Lest thy mind likens to a heart of stone
Liken your voice to the sweet atar of a bird
Strive to be impeccable with your word

Strive to help people ... make that your goal
Bring them together like a large fish shawl
Strive to create happiness whenever you can
Strive always to bring out the best in man

Strive to attain friendship in what e'er you do
'Til loyalty and integrity really shines through
Strive to do good deeds ... make that your goal
Twill reach and touch your very soul

Strive to be kind what e'er comes your way
Strive always to keep the devil at bay
Strive for good intentions in what e'er you do
Above all things ... strive to be true

WORDS

Words can be very painful
One should be careful in what they say
A hurtful expression may be withdrawn
But never e'er forgotten in any way

Spoken words can be used
To gladden the hearts of men
Like the written word in wartime
The sword is less mighty than the pen

In the past decade of centuries
Words have been mailed on pigeon's wings
Carrying enough malice and doom
To condemn and behead reigning kings

So in future – try lookin   hard before you leap
Think carefully before saying yet another word
Let the words flow smoothly, sweet and deep
And become likened to the sweet song of a bird

WORDS (2)

Through your word you exert a creative power
It can build or destroy a life like a wilted flower
A well spoken word can achieve good things like magic
To speak words of malice and vice is tragic

Your word is a force ... a most formidable tool
Can be used to create happiness ... e'er so cool
A word can destroy lives at an expeditious pace
But also restore a soul to a state of grace

Always strive to be impeccable with your word
Be of virtuous character ... let only good words be heard
Words of malice can be harmful ... a terrible thing
Words can be as poisonous as a cobra's sting

Bad words breed nothing but solace and grief
And steals away happiness like a devious thief
Never say a bad thing in anger or spite
It can only cause pain like a tiger's bite

Idle gossip causes nothing but sadness and forlorn
As it only breeds malice, lies and scorn
Speak nothing but the truth as often as you can
It helps to bring out the character in man

Use integrity before saying yet another word
Liken thy message to the melodious sound of a bird

The following poem is about a pilgrimage in Northern Spain which has been ongoing since the 9th century. Millions of pilgrims from all over the world make the arduous journey year after year. I read about it whilst studying Spanish and felt compelled to take on the arduous task.

EL CAMINO DE SANTIAGO DE COMPOSTELA

'Twas during a course at night school
Students were serious and clannish
Learning adjectives, verbs and nouns,
Getting to grips with Spanish

Fred, one of the classmates,
Displayed a festive trend
During our studying
He became my special friend

Part of the course
In order to obtain a pass
We'd to talk for fifteen minutes
In front of the class

It was a difficult task
In fact, I found it a pain
'Cos the speech we had to make
Was in the language of Spain
However, a rule of the criteria
Eased part of the chore
And gave me the confidence
To take to the floor

We could talk about anything
No matter what the theme
My task now seemed much easier
Now, no longer a dream

My chosen thesis
Was about different 'Legends in Spain'
Which in future years to come
Was to see me trudging in torrential rain

I became intrigued with 'El Camino de Santiago',#
Translated - 'The Road of Saint James'
It jumped right out of the pages
Like a sparkling ember in the flames

El Camino de Santiago de Compostela
A pilgrimage in Northern Spain
A course, Federico and I
Traipsed many times oe'r stony terrain
Ongoing since the ninth century
Renowned the whole world over
A route oe'r Pyrenees Mountains
Festooned with woods, fern and clover

Millions of pilgrims take up the challenge
Each and every year
Slogging away carrying heavy backpacks
Smiles on their faces - no sign of fear

Trudging up many steep mountain path,
Plodding on in blistering heat
Aching backs, oozing sweat
Accompanied with blistered feet

An average daily walk for the crusaders
Approximately eighteen to twenty miles per day
Hopefully reaching an albergue
A hostel where they can stay

However, this is not always possible
As 'Albergue esta completo' by far
Depicting that the hostel is full
Only option left - to sleep out under a star

Federico and I became regular adventurers
Kitted out in travelling gear
We became well known on the Camino
Footslogging it year after year

'CAFOD', a renowned charity
Excepted Fred and I into one of its bands
In order to raise sponsor money
For Third World impoverished lands

One time we acted as guides
To a group of fourteen pilgrims or more
The entire group was inexperienced
Making it a rather arduous chore

But the end result was favourable
After traipsing o'er hills and fells
Sufficient funds were used in Africa
To build a new school and water wells

Compostela derived from latin, 'Campus Stellae'
Meaning 'Field of the Star'
Many miracles occurred over the ages
Attracting countless pilgrims from afar

Pilgrims encouraging each other
Over muddy and rocky grounds
Despite being in pain and weary
Happiness and friendships clearly abound

If only this planet of ours
Could liken itself to the 'Camino' free
Beguiling, so full of love and giving
What a wonderful world it would be

HEART LIKE A WILDFLOWER

A wise person is pleasing in God's eyes
His countenance is endowed with special power
It doth glow like twinkling stars in the skies
And is blessed with a heart of a wildflower

Integrity' is ingrained into a wise soul
Even through tormentous gales and rain
After being trampled after a bad fall
He's strong enough to rise up and start again

A wildflower is similar in that respect
After being trampled down into the dust
'Twill rejuvenate itself and re-erect
By nature's law it will up-rise and thrust

THE RIGHT PATH

Modern life can be very frustrating
Striving against all odds to compete
Working all the hours that God sends
In order to make ends meet

Because of poverty a soul of't can be tempted
If a lucrative deal happens his way
A gift fallen off the back of a lorry
Can ease stress and brighten a day

However ... be aware of what comes easy
Even though it appears great at the time
Because in the long run there's always a drawback
And could easily lead to a life of crime

Try always to stay on the right path
Especially living in an era fast and flowing
It's shrewd to know where you are in life
But far more important to know where you're going

A GIFTED VOICE

Like gifted singers of bygone days
Others will come yet to be proclaimed
A soothing voice favoured by the winds
Whose voyage through life has been pre ordained,#
A voice that echoes like an archaic legend
Bound by an incantatory spell
Straight from Empyrean on a billowing cloud
'Twill infiltrate every valley, dale and dell

An aria pleasing to man's ears
Likened to the sweet tones of a psaltery
Enchanting mankind by its sweet cadence
Likened to music of birds in a tree
Listening to Heavenly cantata
Creates a magical effect by and by
One's mind is soothed by its calm melodious sound
As a sweet attar ornaments the sky

AMBIGUOUS

Despite crisis and adversity
Who I am … determined am I to sustain
I can't help being me
As I am … I will remain

Throughout diverse affliction
I will always generously bestow
No matter … the trial or crisis
I'll still remain … status quo

We're only here for a borrowed time
Precious moments not to be wasted
Golden chances buried in the sand
By insight … could've been foretasted

Throughout trials and tribulations of life
I continuously strive to make it my aim
Whether my fate be failure or success
I treat both imposters … exactly the sam

Walkin' amongst gentry … or the downtrodden
Treat them as you would have them treat you
Be fair, be generous … always try to be wise
And throughout your life … you'll keep your virtue

SLANDER

Even though at times my mind doth tend to wander
Ne'er will I lower my standards by subjecting
myself to slander
To slight a man's name can cause nothing but anxiety and
pain
Always judge men as you find them ... strive to make
that your aim

TONGUE

The tongue is likened to a fire
It can create warmth and grace
But can also cause hurt and dire
At a cruel, slow tedious pace

The tongue is small but like a tiny ember
It can be a world of iniquity and malice
So one must be wise and remember
A tiny spark can destroy an emperor's palace

All wild beasts and reptiles can be tamed
But the tongue cannot be subdued by man
Think carefully before a hard word is aimed
Speak words of love whenever thou can

If we put a bit into a horses mouth
We are able to control its entire soul
To steer it north, east, west or south
As though it was a young newborn foal

Great ships are steered by a small rudder
To wherever the steerman wants it to go
'Tis enough to make a soul shake and shudder

A spiteful word causes nought but sorrow and woe
Allow wisdom to sail from thy tongue
Let goodness flow in words of good taste
Lies against the truth is a terrible throng
Integrity is first and foremost chaste

The tongue can be blessed or so very wrong
It can create blessings or a sorrowful bane
Words ought to be as a melodious song
As sweet as honey or sugar cane

A serpent's tongue yields unhappiness and forlorn
It tends to cause misery and terrible wrath
Wisely use words as to the manner born
'Twill help keep thee on the righteous path

The moral is to let wise words be heard
And create happiness though-out all mankind
Strive therefore to achieve the engrafted word
A rarer gift thou wilt never e'er find

IMPARTIALLITY

All men should be treated the same
No matter their status in life
It doesn't matter from whence they came
Treat each as a good husband treats his wife

If a rich man of fine apparel enters a room
As does a poor man in mean attire
Never e'er treat the poor man with gloom and doom
And the wealthy man like a pompous squire

Do not place the rich man in a good seat
And sit the poor man in a corner on a stool
To the gentry this is a typical feat
To the poor gent it is degrading and cruel

A wise man displays his good ways
His behaviour is likened to a sage
Goodness he displays like brilliant rays
Integrity flows freely whatever his age

RICH AND POOR

Since time immemorial ... a great divide 'tween rich and poor
Poor just want to get by ... rich crave for more and more
Destitute communities are close knit ... content with their lot
Should a neighbour fall ill ... help is there on the dot
Hot soup or whatever given with gracious intent
Help around the home ... or anything relevant
Downcast, living from hand to mouth ... sad and oppressed
A serious problem, to which the law should be addressed

Authority need to be wary ... ought to come up with a solution
Or afflicted may rise from the ashes
like the French Revolution
Rich society smugly, living off the fat off the land
Would gladly deprive the poor of anything so grand
Greedy Bankers, in spite of selling the country short
Astonishingly, still receive huge bonuses by award of court
Their policy, 'Keep the needy downtrodden, on the rocks
If they get out of hand ... put them into the stocks

To them, the disadvantaged are a low form of life
No concern shown towards their sadness, misery and strife
Way of thinking ... 'Be in control, great to have the power!
They derive out and out pleasure, able to gloat, jeer and glower
But despite all their trappings, money and wealth
The opulent are not happy people ... a poor
ingredient for health
Carrying on in their wanton ways, immorality cruelty and greed
Not caring about all the indigent mouths they could feed

Millions in the bank, but still striving like drones
Wanting more and more to keep up with the Jones
Unwisely, they're causing themselves nothing but gloom
Like lemmings seeking disaster ... they'll fall to their doom

Unlike their underlings ... they lack a good repartee
Trapped by their gluttony ... they no longer feel free
Hard for them to understand is a poor man's happiness
A legacy, despite all their money, they'll never e'er possess
'If with money ... life you could buy,
The rich would live and the poor would die.

WISDOM (2)

Wisdom is peaceful, docile, kind and giving
And is in enmity against sin with the Lord
It is brighter than a constellatin of stars
And vibrates like a musical chord

Ask for wisdom when you kneel and pray
And God will grant it to thee a plenty
Thy soul wilt be endowed with a vibrant ray
And thy heart will lean towards heaven's entry

Wisdom enriches faith and faith begets tolerance
Patience will steer you towards the good path
It is pleasing to God to ask Him for wisdom
It cleanses thy soul of any kind of wrath

Gather not earthly riches in life or class
They are like clay and for sure wilt not last
The sun's burning heat wilt burn and parch the grass
Like a beautiful flower it shall wilt and pass

Wisdom is an aura of God's light
She reflects his image of integrity and love
An unsullied person's eyes shine e'er so bright
As she abides by the laws from above

A soul is oft' tempted and drawn into sin
But iniquity is of one's own pain
God never tempts from afar or within
A soul's contention is often for profit and gain

A rich man in his poor state is sour
A poor man in his high state is pure
The rich will pass away like a wilted flower
The good poor man's path leads to heaven for sure

Blessed is the tried man, who endures desire
'Tis is a hard task but his gift will be great
Satan is well known as a typical liar
To resist him leads to a heavenly fate

MORALITY

There are so many dawns that have not yet risen
Forgive thy tormentors lest thou be not forgiven
Ye who permits thy neighbour to hunger and thirst
Is hitherto doomed, despised and cursed
Whether or not thou sees the dawn of yet another day
Depends on the role thou hast been chosen to play
Goodness pours its heart out ... even onto wicked things
Giving out a message of hope on angel's wings
A person of good intent radiates divine
Doing fine work with reverence sublime.
Cast away false riches come about by ill begot
For the sun will rise and set when you are not
Never e'er chastise love ones in an anguished tone
Lest thou finds thyself unhappy and all alone
Like a sea urchin basking 'tween surf on a sunny night
Good morality contains no painful word or spite
Strive always to treat thy neighbour with deep respect
And you won't regret it later in retrospect

DEEP ROOTS

A wise man narrated the proverb
'Spare the rod and spoil the child'
Then likened it to nature
About trees growing in the wild

Two young men inherited some farm land
Each received a plot, an acre in size
Both eagerly planted seeds in the soil
Watching over it with special vigilant eyes

One watered his seedlings sparingly
As though leaving them to their own plight
The other was over protective
And watered his plants morning, noon and night

Many years passed by and both plots prospered
Large oaks emerged from the earth
Two glorious orchards of green leaves
An oasis for brand new birth

Both men were proud of their creations
As their branches reached way up to the sky
Giving way for birds and other creatures
To breed and build nests way up high

Alas, along came a formidable draught
That was to last for seven years or more
The trees that had been overly watered
Sadly died and withered to the floor

The poor man was at his wit's end
By the devastation of his trees
Whereas, his young friend's branches
Still fluttered freely in the breeze

He couldn't understand the reason
Why his plants could not survive
Especially as his mate's trees
Were apparently vibrant and alive

"I'm so sorry about your crisis"
Said his mate in a voice true and sincere
But you over watered your plants
The trees that you loved so dear

Whereas I gave mine a bare amount
Just enough to keep them alive
They had to dig their roots way down deep
In order to find more moisture and survive

Sadly, because of your over kindness
Your saplings had no chance at all
You spoiled them, leaving them defenceless
With hardly any roots at all

Just like the biblical proverb
The moral behind this tal,
Is to love thy offspring, but do not spoil
Lest thy child becomes feeble and frail

GOD'S HEAVENS

Long ago, before time e'er began
There existed nothing but cold, emptiness and dark
God didn't like what he saw
And decided to bestow it with his mark

To create a wonderful world was his intent
And to fill it with plants, animals and man
All this he created from nothingness
As only the Almighty can

God simply said, "Let it be so"
And the darkness became a dazzling light,
'Twas the first day since time immemorial
Stars twinkled in the heavens e'er so bright

Amid countless nebulas in the universe
He planted our planet Earth
Begetting seeds of the forest
Giving way for brand new birth

A garden of Eden for all creatures
A truly blessed cause
If only mankind would follow
And keep to all God's wise laws

THE WAY OF LIFE

The secret to true happiness
Is to have a worth-while purpose in life
Busy yourself with a worthy cause
And rid thyself of worry and strife

Integrity rings clear like a crystal ball
And it lights up a person's face
It is pleasing in God's eyes
And infiltrates the soul with grace

Soak up wisdom at every opportunity
Take advice from elderly sages
As they hold the key to many problems
A gift passed down through the ages

No doubt, life can be a struggle
But whatever the challenge may be
Always be true to your inner self
And leave your mind wide open and free

It takes courage to follow your conscience
But listen carefully and do what it right
Never ever compromise yourself for gain
For it will lead to a downhill plight

Brave is the man of integrity
During times of hardship and stress
It takes courage to keep your virtue
But it's a task one must address

Integrity, kindness, fairness and courage
Acquire all these if you possibly can
Act upon the truth and pursue it
A poor man of virtue is indeed a very rich man

To be honest and true to thyself
Is likened to bathing in a cool refreshing lake
It frees the mind of turmoil and stress
Giving wisdom as to the right path you take

As dawn breaks, kneel down and make a vow
Pray for thyself and thy fellowman
If by nightfall you are at peace of mind
Then you have done all that you possibly can

It'll be far better at the end of your days
Rather than seeking money, wealth and fame
If, when you leave this planet Earth
It is a better place than you came
A sure path to anxiety and frustration

Is to strive for wealth and power
Material wealth may accumulate
But the soul becomes surly and dour

THE PATH TO HEAVEN

Let not ye be bad for
the sake of man's fate
Risk not the invitation to heaven's pearly gate
Be of kind soul to mankind, friend or foe
And cast out any doubts of finishing down below
If you don't let the devil in through your front door
He'll strive to work himself under the floor
Or through the skylight in the dead of the night
He'll never give up 'bout a long boisterous fight
There are two roads in life on which one can cruise
The life 'ere after depends on which one you choose
Twinkling stars shine in the heavens above
Dreams in our head … a white dove filled with love
So fly along with the angels to keep evil at bay
And end up a happy soul at the end of the day
The tale's morale is to be good even through trouble and strife
And be welcomed into Heaven at the end of your life

QUOTES FROM SHAKESPEARE

Expressions come from within one's inner self
Pure thoughts cannot be bought with money
Wisdom used in poetic verse
Is likened to nectar and honey
Quotes from William Shakespeare are extremely wise
His idioms are from heaven above
God surely gazed down from the skies
And filled his heart with love

He's the world's most famous playwright
His quotes came from deep within his heart
It was indeed his blessed plight
Others were very good but so very far apart
At times it's hard to come up with a suggestion
But to Shakespeare it came naturally to him
'To be or not to be … that is the question'
It didn't come about by chance, nor on a whim

'All's well that end's well' … another famous quote
'Tis a position, nice to find ourselves in
As true now as on the day that it he wrote.
It feels like having a bit of a win

Another recite so dearly heartfelt and true
'If I lose mine honour, I lose myself'
Integrity is likened to the morning dew
Honour is far richer than money and wealth
Cultivate the soil and plant good seeds
To attain wisdom he gave us a clue
To live a good life ... a life of good deeds
'This above all ... to thine own self be true

'It is not enough to speak, but to speak the truth'
'Tis an expression that dearly touches my heart
Likened to the melodious sound of a flute
Words of wisdom and truth clearly keep men apart
Shakespeare also wrote many a poem
'This England' was one of the best
'Twas consuminate ... 'twas a flawless gem
'Twas absolute put to the ultimate test

Writing poetry can bring out the best in man
Especially from one's inner soul
As long as he does the best that he can
And the work is his own overall

KEEP THE DEVIL AT BAY

Strive always to keep the devil at bay
He'll wield his power to steal your soul
Offer you the world to get his own way
And undermine your virtue like a burrowing mole

He'll traipse o'er marshland or through a dense wood
He's canny and devious, and e'er so bright
He'll play on your pride and make you feel good
And convince you that everything wrong is right.

If you don't let him in through a window
He's sure to come in through a door
Through a skylight in the dead of the night
Or work his way under your floor

Don't e'er fall for a promise of silver and gold
Or an assurance of property and wealth
You'll eventually be left out in the cold
A poor ingradient for sanity and health

TONGUE (2)

The tongue can be the very word if iniquity
Or it can be ever so soothing and kind
It can be restless, evil and full of deadly poison
Or indeed a blessing to guide and uphold mankind
Out of the mouth comes blessings and curses
These things need not be necessarily so
Speak venom and cause nought but sadness and grief
Whereas words of kindness maketh the heart glow

Does a fountain spill out forth sweet and bitter water
Can a fig tree bear olives or a vine figs
So neither can salt water yield fresh water
Cast not thy tongue into the language of pigs
Show wisdom by thy good behaviour
Never e'er be liars against the truth
Thy tongue can be earthy, sensual and devilish
Many downfalls and successes are its proof

The moral behind the use of the tongue
Be diligent and use words kind and fair
Bad words cause nought but heartache and pain
Whereas kind words display affection and care

FATE OF THE RICH

Rich people are blinded by their wealth
Unaware of miseries yet to come
Their riches wilt rot away into the dust
And their garments will be moth-eaten and numb

The gold and silver wilt condense and rust
And the rust shalt be a witness against their goal
The very material things which they coveted
Shall declare the wickedness of their soul

They laid up treasure during their lifetime
And feasted on the fruits of the earth
They nourished theirs heart in dissipation
And caused misery and strife with all their worth

At the end of their glorious days
Fire will flare up and engulf their flesh
Their cries wilt be heard throughout the earth
As they are cast deep down into a fiery mesh.

LITTLE WHITE STONES

I wonder if you've ever noticed
Whilst strolling on a tarmac path
Tiny white specks of light
Reflecting light back up from the black
These little specks are white stones
They are part of the tarmac mix
Their function ... to hold the alloy together
And give it a permanent fix

Tarmac alone wouldn't last long in the elements
It would crack, crumble and shift
Dirt, weeds and grass would insert
Causing the weak blend to lift
Tarmac envelops the small pebbles
With a strong and warm embrace
The object of the small white stones
Is to hold everything in its place

Without stones ... cracks would lengthen and widen
Enabling the growth of grassy crops
However ... within a stony mixture
When a crack hits a stone, it stops!

Liken the white stones in the tarmac
To an incredible work of art
A little light in the darkness
Stops everything from falling apart

THE ELEMENTS

The wind blows wildly spreading nutrients and seeds
Enabling creatures to attain special needs
As a gust blows it creates swirling leaves
As a river flows it ebbs and weaves
Trees strong and stout at their ultimate test
Are a habitat where wild birds build their nests
Mountains store water in their mighty frame
Later to cascade down a craggy lane
Clouds soak up water from the deep blue sea
Later to fall as rain o'er a grassy lea
Lush grass grows on barren land and plains
Food to wild animals and long legged cranes
The sun shines bright o'er sea and sand
Creating life even in desert lands
Its rays infiltrate the entire earth
Strengthening body and soul like a horse's girth
Mother Nature prevails through hail, rain and snow
Each season she displays her own unique show
At times she appears to put on frown
But she will never e'er let us down.

I AM A CLOUD

I reside in the heavens way high in the sky
Taking in beautiful vistas as I float by and by
I oft' burst open into streaming showers
A gift to buds of thirsting flowers
As my wings open I awaken the dew
Grasslands spring to life with a glorious hue
Many creatures abound 'neath earthy soil
New life springs to life throughout turmoil and toil

During torrential storms and relentless gales
I unleash rain onto countless hills, woods and dales
I float about in the heavens gazing down at the earth
And smile as water gives way to new birth
Young chicks hatch out in a leafy nest
Gently cuddled and loved nigh to mother's breast
Creatures survive by hard work and plunder
Even 'tween bouts of exuberant thunder.

To celebrate I oft' put on a glorious display
My way of thanking earth for a glorious day.
As day is closing I oft' entwine with a red sky at night
And become part of a most beautiful, heavenly sight.

RIVER

Nothing is more enduring than a river's plight
As it flows constantly day and night
Its trek across continents ... it ends never
For its relentless task goes on forever
To splash and crash like a band of rebels
It carves out rock and stone into magnificent pebbles
Creatures abound as it adheres to nature's wish
By supplying nutrients to wildlife and fish
Slowly through every nook and cranny it goes
Creating a life giving source wherever it flows
'Tis a God given aqueous from way up high
Working alongside billowing clouds in the sky
It twists and turns like a gigantic snake
Pouring out goodness within its wake
Thankfully its task doth go on forever
And its magnificent feat will end ... never

LAUGHTER

Laughter is a good thing ... it helps to lift the spirit high
It tends to keep grief at bay and happiness nigh
When a soul is laughing, happiness is in the air
'Tis a soothing touch so fine and fair
'Tis impossible to be sad when laughter doth abound
Only good feelings are attained when it is around
In that fleeting moment 'tis unfeasible to be sad
Cast away are any thoughts sad or bad
Like a beautiful flower bursting to bud
A bout of laughter creates nothing but good
An ancient proverb to use as your cue
Laugh and the entire world laughs with you
The moral behind this tale is to make laughter your goal
And nature's special gift will embrace your very soul

A SONG

The Lord gave us a body enabling us to sing

'Tis a marvellous gift ... 'tis a God given thing

Sing in your kitchen ... sing in the shower

Your mind will blossom like a beautiful flower

Sing in fields, leas, hills and dales

Sing even in windy and gusty gales

Sing to the moon and the stars in heaven

And ride the wind on cloud Lucky Seven

Sing to people you don't even know

'Twill allay all your fears and fill you with awe

Sing to yourself ... a joy to behold

And a beautiful vale will start to unfold

Whatever you chose to sing doesn't matter at all

Yet a spiritual feeling will encompass your soul

A NEW DAY

I awoke this morning to a dawn chorus
The sound of birds singing in a tree
The sweet harmonic sounds touched my soul
And filled my entire being with glee
As I listened to the beautiful sounds
I began to realise their ploy
Their goal was to filtrate the air with music
And to fill my heart with joy

The little creatures don't ask for much
Scrapings of food, a tree branch on which to rest
Watery spots, green leaves and twigs
An old building or a tree where they can nest
To us mere mortals it would be unbearable
We just couldn't live like that
But to those adorable creatures
To them it's a sweet, beguiling habitat

I love how these tiny creatures
Accept all life's turbulence and strife
The way they ask for nothing more
Than the bare necessities of life

My love of wildlife comes to me from within

It's a rudiment I enjoy,

I love all creatures in my tenth decade

Just the same as when I was a boy

A MOTHER'S LOVE

A mother's always there, no matter what
Even in times of disappointment and despair
With a warm heart and healing hands
She offers comfort with a love so very rare
When a loved one is feeling lonely and downcast
Her warmth flows freely creating harmony and peace
Wrapping a magic cloak around her family
With a love that will ne'er cease
She teaches how to face up to life's problems
And not to go about grasping life's sultry pleasures
But how to seek out what really matters
Natures beguiling ways and exotic earthly treasures
She nurtures and plants seeds of wisdom
Deep down into the realms of our heart
With unselfish devotion from a spirit within
In soul and body she doth become a part
A mother's love surely is a blessing
Of this there is no doubt
Unconditional, boundless, unselfish love
Is what she's all about!

ACHIEVEMENT

A man can achieve anything if he decides to do it
Nothing on earth more pliable than the human spirit
Mother Nature plays her part from the day we are born
Building up resilience through pestilence and storm
Keep up your pecker ... it lifts your heart and mind
Face problems head on ... e'en when life appears unkind
Go boldly forward ... strive to climb the highest hill
And slow but sure ... hopes and dreams you surely will fulfil
Look to the night sky ... let the heavens be your guide
Earn the right ... shoulders back, head held high with pride

STOP THE WANTING

Traipsing wild open moorland, mere mortals frozen to the bone
Elements likened to Tundra, a vast icy treeless zone
Yet feral birds hover in the heavens flying e'er so free
Taking life as it comes day by day, enjoying nature's tranquillity
Wild creatures of every species with a life of no length to measure
Foraging endlessly for food ... browsing at their leisure
Unburdened by the thoughts of man. Exhibiting awesome splendour
Accepting nature's tacit plan, succumbing to life's agenda
If only man could but take note of animals oh so free
No more want, just need ... what a happy world this would be

PUSH AND SHOVE

Through troubled times of push and shove
Try to help even those you find difficult to love
Obtain a good attitude each and every day
Lest thou should slip, falter and go astray
Tribulations ... a cause of misery, grief and strife,
Gnaw away constantly throughout our life.
Tackle each problem in the best way you can
To do a job well brings out the character of man
Peace and happiness cannot come about
Without a little wear and tear
These special qualities are achieved
With tender love and care

NATURAL BEAUTY

Even in bedlam or chaos

Tranquillity and peace can be found

If only one would take in

All the grace and beauty that abounds

Breathe in nature's pure living air

Give the heart a chance to respond

Let your body spring to life

Like the flowers on a lily pond.

One day I was lucky enough to come across a wild bush that was full of tiny red admirals. I was so taken aback by their unique design and outstanding beautiful natural colours that I felt I needed to put my feelings into verse

A RED ADMIRAL

A most beautiful creation of nature
Entrancing in every minute detail
Adorned in splendour and enticing colours
Sleek ad tender from head to tail
Fluttering 'mongst plants and flowers
I was fortunate to espy
The most fragile delicate creature
A beautiful, red admiral butterfly

It flitted 'mongst a myriad of flowers
Each one with its own unique hue
Camouflaged amongst a cluster of red roses
A contrast 'tween plants green and blue
As it browsed fro' flower to flower
Its fragile wings glistened in the sun
A most tantalising scenario ne'er has been
Startling colours intermingled into one

It continued to flutter 'round a hedgerow
Never e'er faltering for a rest
It put me in mind of a parent bird
Flying back and forth from its nest
To espy a red admiral is enchanting
Its movements so exquisitely sublime
A tacit plan by Mother Nature
Since an epoch of geological time

It seems a pity that something so gorgeous
Has been endowed with such a short lifespan
Yet it goes about its daily chores
Giving untold pleasure to man

Whilst walking beside a river I picked up a tiny pebble. Looking at it closely I noticed how beautiful it was.

JEWEL IN THE CROWN

'Tis orange, blue, red and yellow
Tinted with a touch of white, grey and brown
Adorned with all the colours of the rainbow
'Twould befit an emperor's crown
Temperedand sculptured in fast flowing rivers
Or by an ocean of incessant tides
Washed ashore by white capped water
In the crest of a wave it slides
I'm in awe as I gaze at its structure
'Tis a thing so complex … so marvellously made
Moulded by the elements of nature
No earthy human could achieve such grade
No artist's brush could ever emulate its colours
Intermingled with white, turquoise and gold
As the sun hits its smooth satin finish
Lights of sparkling beauty unfold
What is this object of such exquisite beauty?
'Tis a stone that can be found in the sand
Also on river beds and mountain trails
'Tis a stone … 'tis a pebble in my hand!

MAGNIFICENT EAGLE

Many birds fly high on thermals ... an uplift of warm air

But the eagle is different with its own elegant flair

Reaching great heights o'er mountains, a technique of its own

By riding upon stormy winds with a rare, gentle tone

High in the heavens, beholding below, a magnificent view

'Neath a dazzling sun, a painted azure sky e'er so blue

It spreads out its large magnificent wings

To make its effortless flight

To watch any bird in flight is magical

But to espy an eagle ... is to behold a wonderful sight

ETERNITY

Strolling on a beach one day
I scooped up a handful of sand
'Twas impossible to count the grains
As they lie millions in my hand
Gazing along the sandy beach
It disappeared into a far distant shore
It got my mind to thinking
How many trillions of tiny grains more?
There are countless beaches and deserts
Scattered around the globe in far distant lands
And many undiscovered nooks and crannies
Hiding hoards of salt gritty sands
If every one of these grains
Represented a hundred years or more
'Twould add up to zillions of years
A complicated mind boggling score
A time too vast for humankind to comprehend
As it seems to go on into infinity
Yet to God ... it is but a fleeting moment
Compared to Eternity

A HARD WORKING MAN

A hardworking soul has integrity
And is a credit to mankind,
His laborious deeds profit his neighbours
A more worthy character is hard to find.

A man working conscientiously
To achieve the best he can,
Show me a man, happy in his work
And I will show you a happy man.

Laze about and wait for things to happen
And gradually you will find'
A field cannot be ploughed
By simply turning it over in your mind.

WEATHER.

When the weather's unsettled and tedious
And life appears rather mundane,
Take a look at it with different eyes
Even in an outburst of thunderous rain.

The world is full of charm and adventure
Much beauty to take in and behold,
But to find all the allure and speculation
One's got to act audacious and bold.

Whether a day be bright or tempestuous
Take advice from a busy bumble bee,
Take in all the beautiful scenes around you
It's surprising how much you will see.

We can't cast aside life's daily problems
Our dilemmas, trouble and strife,
But by taking in God's natural beauty
'Twill lead to a much happier life.

SPRINGTIME.

My mind drifts back to when I was a child
Adoring the outdoors. savouring nature's wild
To feel fresh wind in my face, to watch clouds drifting by
Enthralled by the tranquillity of an azure blue sky
A painting no artist could capture, rays of sunshine breaking through
Defusing 'mongst trees and moorland, and grassy morning dew
All the allure enveloped me, a joy for my eyes to see
To explain in written words would take eternity

Springtime, a happy era, birds singing e'er so free
Endowing all the countryside with an air of tranquillity
It seems to be nature's tacit plan using sunshine and rain
No matter where e'er you be, plants spring to life again
Every season has its special features but one explicit aspect of spring
Leaves reappear on trees and flowers start blossoming
Sunshine and April showers encompass all the earth
Encouraging plants to grow, giving way for brand new birth

Carpets of flowers cover hills and dales exhibiting life anew
Each tiny petal, its own unique colour with a finer deeper hue
Demure closed buds start to respond, succumbing to nature's agenda
Disencumbered, they spring to life, displaying exotic splendour

Nothing in the world could e'er be more enchanting or so fair
Than daffodils or tulips in their short span of energy and flair
Elegant scenery doth our very eyes affect conveying other life abounds
Sweet twittering of tiny nestling birds and additional intriguing sounds

Spring is a joyous era as once again she starts her reign
And, but for a short spell her majesty shall be queen again
To capture the magic of spring-time whether it be
a flower or a tree
It would have to be written by a far wiser scribe than me

UNIVERSE DISPLAYED

I oft' wonder at the miracle of life
How creatures struggle on through hardship and strife
How people wonder what it's all about
Whilst others have faith without any doubt
I myself know it is a gift from God
Created by His divine celestial rod
To dwell in a world e'er so pure and divine
With beautiful landscapes unaltered by time

I gaze at the clouds in awesome wonder
Lightning flashes across the heavens midst bouts of thunder
Water cascades down hills, mountains and a forest glade
'Tis nature's way of the universe displayed
After the storm follows a glorious paradise
Many winged creatures adorn beautiful blue skies
Birds singing sweetly in nesting trees
One can hear brooks and feel a nice gentle breeze

Life abounds in lofty mountains grandeur
Carpeted in snow e'er so white and land pure
Animals forage for their young with love
All brought about by The Lord above

The stars in the heavens shine e'er so bright
The moon and the sun provide heat and light
Not for a moment, in God, have I not believed
As the universe displays His heavenly creed
And so the way I look at it
All my organs are healthy and fit
God created my body and gave me life
And helps me to cope with toil and strife

Then again, I've always loved nature overall
As it touches my senses and my very soul
God willing I will never e'er be dismayed
And constantly soak up universe displayed.

Although my last poem is not about nature or biblical I enclose it because to me it is about real life and the way that friendship is formed. The era was during the 1940's.

JUNIOR SCHOOL

St Thomas's was the name of our school
All the kids were poor but e'er so cool
Wearing steel-bottom clogs that made a great sound
We created bright sparks by kicking the ground
At nine on the dot into single file we fell
The marched into class to the sound of a bell
Paraded like soldiers dressed in our clogs
Clip clop, clip clop went the sound of our clogs
At playtime we used to play in a yard
I soon learned I had to be hard
The yard was concrete and much to my plight
In that very yard I had my first fight
Sparks from clogs, shouts and jeers
Left many a black eye filled wi' tears
'Twas a hard life but not quite so cruel
No kicking … no biting … we all stuck to the rule
Life is quite strange and through all that strife
Lots of us kids became friends for life

THE SEA.

A quiet still belies the mighty ocean
A calm hush assails a deep labyrinth,
White capped waves splash gently o'er rolling sands
Creating an air of tranquillity and indifference.

Natural elements effect fathoms below
Way down deep on the ocean floor,
Wave after wave of crimson mantles
Gracefully splash every inland shore

This special lady bestows many treasures
Around the globe to exotic far off lands,
She adorns boundless shorelines and beaches
With beautiful pristine, white silvery sands.

She supplies nutrients to mountains and valleys
To great lakes and dry arid lands,
And forms gorgeous life giving oasis's
In vast hot parched desert sands.

Without a doubt, her majesty is giving
And confers all her gifts with a smile,
But woe betide any misgivings
She can be tempestuous angry and vile.

Tsunamis and gale force raging storms
Can destroy lands in the blink of an eye,
And yet mankind is so blind in his thinking
Never e'er stopping to ask the reason why?

A CORAL REEF

Trillions of minute aqueous creatures

Drifting in deep underlying currents of the deep

Destined to end their simplistic life

As a dazzling, colourful, deep coral reef.

To form an exotic beautiful pattern

Nature's tacit plan surely is their blessed fate

A structure of many intricate alluring colours

No earthy artist could e'er emulate.

GOD'S LOVE

The path to heaven is hard and strenuous
But this may not be necessarily so
By living by God's commandments
Good deeds of honesty and kindness will flow

God created all of us in His own image
And He loves us with the whole of His heart
He sent His only son down amongst us
And Jesus became a blessed part

All that is necessary for evil to thrive
Is that good men do nothing at all
'Tis a quote written by a wise man's drive
And we should all respond to its heavenly call

HAVE COURAGE

The hallmark of courage during our life
Is the will to stand by the truth
Determination to be true through trouble and strife
And to back up your mark with definite proof
A man of character will back up his belief
No matter what e'er is thrown at him
He'll remain true through trouble and grief
And strive for the truth no matter how grim

To have a purpose and a true goal in life
Tis a mission or a calling worth living
Like a flower it will blossom throughout strife
Like the sun it will be warm and giving
Do what you believe in and live by it
Abide by the ways of integrity and truth
Steer well clear of an evil man's pit
Let good deeds be your honour and proof

We are not bound to be successful and win
But we are bound to be honest and true
Strive always to avoid the snares of sin
And to end up sweet as a flower's hue

We don't get to choose when we will die
But we certainly get the chose how to live
So one should walk with head held high
And their love and kindness generously give

BE YOURSELF

Always try to be the person you are
You are the person whom The Lord has made
Your life is as bright as a shining star
And sparkles like a sunny mountain glade
Be true to thyself and speak from the heart
Don't compromise for you are all that you've got
Your life is precious so play your part
No matter what happens, give it your lot

No matter how many times you may stumble or fall
Pick thyself up and hold your head up high
Learn by your mistakes, make that your goal
And you will gradually prosper by and by

A HARD WORKER

'Tis important to know where we are in life
But more- to know where we are going
Make it your goal to keep kindness rife
For it tends to keep the spirit up and flowing
To attain a nature like a mature sweet wine
Always do a day's work as best you can
Satisfaction in a chore is a gift divine
It helps to bring out the best in man

Work can be love in action or deed
And if more people made it a heavenly chore
Friendships would flourish like a blessed seed
And people would accomplice much more
Put thy heart into everything you do
Strive always to give it your very best
Liken thy work to the morning dew
Like a bird gathering twigs for its nest

If at the end of a working day
You have done everything you can
There's no way you will keep sleep at bay
For thou hast kept to God's heavenly plan

Work hard, play hard and make it fun
For work does not have to be a chore
Enjoy it like basking 'neath a warm sun
And benefits will enhance more and more

NATURE IS BEHOLDING

Strolling through open green countryside
Is good for my body, mind and soul
As I listen to a voice in the wind
It makes me feel fresh, alive and whole

Soothing music fills me with strength and wisdom
Especially when I'm feeling kind o' low
A sensational tingling embraces me
And my whole countenance starts to glow

May I always embrace Nature's beauty
And envisage raindrops o'er a Scottish loch
To be able to unlock the secrets
Of what lies underneath each leaf and rock

I long to stroll through a tropical forest
And absorb all the beauty I can get
To take in the fragrance of Nature
Before my life wanes likes a fading sunset

SELF AWARENESS

Throughout my life I have been blessed to see
Many graces and the rapture of nature's company
Eternally, alfresco has me enthralled and nurtured like a child
Naught more enchanting- than to be in cosmos wild
To feel the wind in my face ... to see an azure sky so blue
To walk through luscious green grass ... sparkling with morning dew
To listen to frogs croaking or the sweet sound of singing birds
Deep inner feelings aroused ... impossible to put into words
Breathe in nature's fresh air, enjoy ... this is my cue
Appreciate a flower's fragrance ... each with
its own distinguished hue
Acknowledge the circle of life ... as sure as day follows night
If you'll but look around ... many things so bright
Our time on Earth is borrowed ... impossible to measure
Take advantage, each moment ... an elegant treasure
The most learned scribe cannot capture bliss as
the skylark sings
Take advantage – self awareness ... of all nature's wonderful things

IN MY GARDEN

Working the land with its earthy hue
'Neath an azure clear sky e'er so blue
Watching a flower flutter in the breeze
No better place to feel at ease
Songs of Nature with a tune so clear
Nothing more soothing to the human ear
Many intriguing sounds echoing 'round the earth
Creating a feeling of peace and mirth
Everywhere around ... an abundance of life
Tiny insects coping with toil and strife
Ants scurrying hither and thither ... all o'er the place
Soldier ants overlook ... setting the pace
A spider weaving its home ... a fine intricate web
A beautiful pattern of sleek silvery thread
Worms transform dead plants, buds and leaves
And furrow the soil allowing it to breathe
Hard and laborious pulling out weeds
Joyful and rewarding, planting new seeds
Puts me in mind of angels on the day of wrath
Sorting out souls ... the wheat from the chaff
Listening to birds singing in harmonic ease
An abundance of perpetual peace
Watching a bee as it flits from rose to rose
The mind drifts into a state of sweet repose

Deep thoughts ... taking things into account
If my mind is troubled and problems amount
When I'm looking for peace and harmony
My garden is the special place I like to be

MAGIC

As children we used to play in a make do den
And our minds wandered off to a far away glen
Are there such things as magic, pixies and elves?
Do fairies really exist we would ask ourselves
Of course they do my little sister would say
Fairy Tinkerbell and Daisy visit me every day
What do you mean – I asked my mind now alert
My curiosity aroused … I scooped up some dirt
Be careful with that … it's stardust you know
The fairies use it to make flowers grow
It seeps into the ground to feed all the trees
A favourite spot for the birds and the bees
They sprinkle it high into the air
Creating the weather … windy and fair
The elements mix … the moon blooms at night
Brightening the dark … creating some light
With the coming of dawn the sun starts to shine
Giving life to the wheat, the corn and the vine
Its rays filter the fields, rivers and wood
Enabling each plant to blossom and bud
Fairies may not exist …which I think is tragic
But the wonder of nature is truly magic

THE BEAUTY OF MOTHER EARTH

Throughout 'Mother Earth' -... so many wondrous sights
From the lowest depths to far outstanding heights
Majestic snow-capped mountains ... e'er so sublime
Spectacular magical vistas ... unaltered by time

Outstanding beauty of a mountain pass
With snowy crests sparkling like glass
Proud glistening peaks lying in their wakes
Mirrored way below by stunning blue lakes

In life giving water ... many a creature abounds
Begetting enticing and ... the most beautiful sounds
A bountiful oasis ... a paradise
A wonderful haven ...for small field mice

The sound of a woodpecker tapping at a tree
Complimented by the gentle humming of a bumble bee
Within soil or under a stone ... signs of nature abound
Even in barren deserts ... natural beauty can be found

Flowers stand proud ... as though telling a story
'Neath an azure blue sky in all their glory
Mother Nature spreads her colourful cloak way
across the land

Ne'er could an earthy mortal paint anything so grand
Wild plants in the out-backs cast a vibrant hue
Morning beauty ... sparkles in the shimmering dew
Towering hilltops with cascading falls
Green vegetation on sheer cliff walls

Waterfalls giving off a vaporous spray
Composing a most glittering display
Countless stars in the heavens twinkle each night
No precious jewel or gem ... could e'er be so bright

Birds in the woodland ... flying to and fro
Dropping seeds 'bout the land ... helping plants to grow
A soft breeze... slender ferns lazily sway in the mist
Gently embracing each other ... as though two lovers kissed

In winter, Jack Frost leaves many skilful silver lines
Clinging to plants and bushes ... by slender thread designs
At the first sign of light ... e'en before day's begun
Beads of crystal glisten ... in the early morning sun

Tropical forests provide life cover to beast wild and fare
Giving sanctuary to lion ... and the brown grizzly bear
Showers rain down ... from the heavens above
Begetting life ...with an abundance of love

A FOREST

Weathering the elements ... windy and fair
A forest of trees in a woodland glade
Home to many creatures ... big cats and grizzly bear
Offering sanctuary 'neath its leafy shade

Pine trees with girths so vast and wide
Boughs so strong reaching way up high
Birds nestling their young chicks with pride
In nests that almost reach the sky

Tigers, snow leopards and other wild beasts
Mark their territory on a piece of tree bark
A subtle warning to other predators
To be aware ... the enforcer has left its mark

Way up within a tropical opening
Wild gorillas forage for their young
Way down below on the forest floor
Beetles feed on elephant dung

Butterflies posses special dainty features
Beautiful intricate colours ... yellow, red and blue
As they gracefully flutter from flower to plant
Each one with its own unique hue

A habitat for rabbits, elk and deer
Frogs, lizards, snakes and mice
Not just a home for these forest creatures
But a tiny slice of Paradise

IMAGINATION

Imagine the close of a hot summer's day
Stars a twinkling and the moon starts to loom
Atmosphere vibrantly fresh and clean
The sweet attar of a crimson rose in bloom

Imagine a majestic oak tree tall and strong
From a tiny acorn ... it has surpassed its test
Home to countless creatures sheltered by its leafy bough
How many tiny chicks have flown the nest?

Imagine lily white clouds in the heavens
A gleaming raindrop stirred by a soft breeze
The shimmering beauty of multiple colours
A red admiral fluttering 'tween verdant trees

Imagine a soft breath of wind
As it stirs corn and pastures new
And a reflected moon quivers and trembles
Upon a rippling pond in waters blue

Imagine a garden adorned with flowers
And how many seeds still remain inside
Awaiting their short span of life on earth
To exhibit exquisite beauty ... bursting with pride

Imagine birds singing in harmonic ease
Watching bees flitting from rose to rose
An abundance of perpetual peace
A state of calm and sweet repose

Imagine all these beautiful things
A garden of Eden yet to be
It is a bounty well within our grasps
If only we would, but open our eyes ... and see!

CIRCLE OF LIFE

No matter where in the world you be
Natural beauty can be found
Mother Nature spreads her enchanting cloak
O'er each and every ground

Flowers prosper in the morning sun
Many petals do unfold
Magically transforming a barren landscape
Into a carpet of silver and gold.

All the colours of the rainbow
Spring up throughout the land
Magnificent shrubs and trees appear
Sculptured by Nature's hand

Because of this fruitful splendour
Each creature on earth doth arrive
The secret ingredient being water
Without it ... nothing could e'er survive

This precious commodity seeps every corner
Irrigating land ... near and far
Life springs forth ... e'er so vibrant
Twinkling like a shining star

For creatures to exist at all
Water simply has to be rife
Without it ... nothing could e'er survive
As it is the very source of life

It is nature's life giving aqueous
Of this ... there is no doubt
But to reach every nook and cranny
How does this come about?

The blue seas and the oceans
Store life in abundance ... within their wake
Giving rise to brooks and rivers
And every stunning mountain lake

The basin of each ocean
Is full to the very brink
But the mixture is far too salty
Making it impossible to drink

As the sun beats down on the deep seas
Vapour rises up to the clouds
Which in turn floats around the heavens
Covering the Earth in billowing shrouds

This process acts like a filter
Refining water and making sure
It is now fit for consumption
Free from toxins and completely pure

Lightning, wind and other elements
Put on a fantastic show
Clouds then burst wide open
Creating icy rain and sleeky snow

Thick snow falls on the tall peaks
Blanketing pinnacles far and wide
Water seeps into porous elevations
Creating sponges within the mountainside

Throughout the entire elevated range
North, south, east and west
Water is ponderously released
From deep within each colossal crest

Water cascades down sheer craggy walls
And thunders down steep rocky ravines
Driving ferocious through hard solid rock
Carving out awesome deep inner caverns

On its trek ... tributaries unite together
To form large rivers and lakes
Begetting gorges and grand canyons
By undermining solid rock 'til it breaks

The arduous journey ... forward and onward
Doggedly reaches its true destiny
The wide open spaces of the ocean
And the expanse of the deep blue sea

During this fantastic complex journey
The entire planet is showered with rain
Mother Nature kicks in relentlessly
And the process starts all over again

PENDLE HILL

'Twas a mixed day when I started to climb
Elements of sunshine, wind and rain
But it turned out a memory sweet and sublime
Well worth all my striving and pain

Whilst climbing fro' Barley side of Pendle Hill
O'er countryside of beauty and treasure
Wild life creatures gave me a thrill
Wide open countryside added to my pleasure

I loved the view of valleys and dales
It sure got my heart a-beating
I love the sound of blustering gales
And the sound of sheep a-bleating

From my cosy nick I did espy
From a billowing cloud an illuminated glow
A brilliant sun lit up the sky
Putting on a vibrant dazzling show

Standing out proudly on Pendle's mighty chest
Hair like trees with leaves of heather
Blowing wildly 'neath its tawny crest
Rays still twinkling in stormy weather

A mist appeared like a billowing white shroud
But it didn't stay around to linger
It disappeared 'neath a rainy cloud
And slithered off like a snakelike finger

On reaching the top I had to rest
Captured by views of ecological time
An artist's paradise at its best
A scene so serene and e'er so sublime

Overhanging sallows and a ne'er ending green
Wildlife hopping about far and nigh
A more tranquil scene ne'er has been
Birds fluttering and singing in the sky

A sound not heard within a town
Awesome music of dapple crickets
Vibrating 'mongst briar and down
Hopping about like falling wickets

As I sat quietly 'mongst briar and leaves
I felt vibrant and e'er so at peace
T'was a feeling that only silence eaves
As all my tensions it did release

Peering down a green valley I viewed many trees
And my day was almost done
Flailing branches quietly in the evening breeze
I set off down 'neath a setting sun

On my way down I picked up a tiny leaf
It was dainty with a thin like stem
I was amazed by its beautiful sheaf
'Twas a jewel, a gem ... a little diadem

Pendle hill has a fable about witches
Who once dwelled 'tween crannies and ditches
If arrested before their foreseeable wake
Tried and tested and burnt on a stake

Despite this incredible legend
The open moor land appears to go on for ever
People still climb to see Pendle in all its glory
Will they ever stop? I would say never!

I'M SO LAZY

My fellow workers oft' have me on
I'm so lazy ... I take the most pain
But it don't bother me none
'Cos at th'end oft' day ... I've everythin' to gain

Workin' at ten to dozen
Has never e'er appealed to me
Plodding on at a snail's pace
Leaves mi' mind wide open and fancy free

In response to the fast workin' chaps
I'm so lazy I take the most pain
My idea is to get it right first time
Then I don't have to do it all o'er again

FUTURE PAST AND PRESENT

Life is a puzzle made up of chapters three
One is Past ... Two is Present ... Three is yet to be
The past lies behind us ... 'tis a time we cannot change
Can we honestly say ... we've done everything within our range?

Have we done our best for the good of mankind's sake
Or blundered on to see how much money we could make
'Tis now in the present, mistakes can be changed around
An opportune moment to plant new seeds in the ground

Of the future we know nothing ... absolutely nothing at all
So strive now to make it better ... strive to make
that your goal!

I enclose the next two poems to show how friendly persuasion can be very helpful.

LEARN YOUR ABC'S

Young children in a classroom so easily get bored
Making it rather tiresome to learn their ABC's
But a mystic lady teacher ... well aware of this
Created a happy atmosphere by using magical keys

"I am the queen of letters," she informed the entire class
"And I can make all your dreams come true
But first of all children ... you have to believe in me
And that's a very easy thing to do!"

She then opened a golden casket
And out popped letters big and small
Some clambered onto childrens' desks
Others spelt out words on the classroom wall

The wise lady had letters dancing
And they formed lots of happy words
Kittens, puppies, flowers, laughter
And the names of tropical birds

The children called upon the letters
Realising they could do almost anything
Fly around heaven 'mongst far distant stars
Or dance in Wonderland 'round a fairy ring

Boys became hunters in an African jungle
Girls settled for being a nurse
But they all thoroughly enjoyed the lesson
Putting letters together in verse

At first it didn't come easy
And they made words of twos and threes
But they gradually got the hang of it
And mastered their ABC's

VOWELS AND CONSONANTS

Vowels are important characters of the alphabet

Used in all words old and new

They are the five special letters

A - E - I - O - U

All words need to contain a vowel

But that's not strictly true

There is one letter, unique in its own right

It's a consonant, but can be used as a vowel too

To put the record straight

The character is the letter Y

It can be used in two or three letter words

For example ... by, shy or sky

So next time you're doing a crossword

And you're finding it difficult to get by

Stop looking for that elusive vowel

And try checking the letter Y

RAINFORESTS

A jungle of pine, teak, elm or oak
Habitat for creatures wild and free
An ideal nesting place for birds
Monkeys swing freely from tree to tree
The canopy of the tree tops
With boughs adorned in green and red
Forever casting fruit and leaves
The forest floor is carpeted

Rain forests are abundant around the Globe.
Removing toxic gases from the air
Replacing it with an oxygen robe
With ingredients pure and fair
Man should act like the wild beast of the forest
And treat our woodlands with a deep respect
Or for certain he'll regret it later
Looking back in retrospect

THE FOUR SEASONS.

No Scribe could ever capture ... all the seasons e'er so fair
To describe in words ... impossible ... each one so very rare
Beguiling as new life abounds ... all the joys of Spring
Tulips and daffodils ... designing their unique festive ring
As Spring showers arrive ... replacing an icy snowflake
Hibernating creatures from winter's sleep start to awake
Leaves reappear on trees airing extrinsic splendour
Young lambs in grassy leas respond to nature's agenda
Dawns the month of April, raindrops fall from the sky
Transformation from caterpillar to beautiful butterfly
Birds flying to and fro from land to nest
Catering for chicks with nature's nutrients best

Summer sun, high in the sky ... dazzling beams lengthening day
Multi coloured shrubs upended, displaying nature's way
Wasps buzzing around ... busy bees cannot wait
To intermingle 'mongst plants ... many flowers to pollinate
Richly wooden hills hug river banks, e'er so serene
Wild flowers carpet lush meadows, intermingling with green
A time for strolling, cycling or simply lazing about

Swimming, sunbathing ... fishing for trout
In woodland 'neath trees, nettles and briar
Relaxing at night 'round a wooden log camp fire

Looking at it wistfully... the Fall assumes to sport a frown
Flowers, plants and large shrubs appear to close down
Leafless trees, briars withered and bare
Yet beauty abounds ... with a festive elegant flair
Throughout entire countryside ... leaves falling from trees
Carpets of golden brown .... a fresh Autumn breeze
Walking through crisp leaves scattered all o'er the ground
So soothing and calming ... a quaint rustling sound
Nothing more relaxing ... meandering on a cold sunny day
Breathing air so pure ... heart filled with a vibrant ray

Snow, ice and fleece ... intermittent bouts of rain
Jack Frost reappears on the scene once again
A sparkling frost laden tree like a lady in state
Nothing more beautiful ... only nature could emulate
Christmas, a happy time ... bringing families together
Love, happiness, heart warming ... despite cold snowy weather
White covered hills and dales ... time for nature to rest

A painting no artist can capture ... beauty at its very best
Wearing its seasonal coat ... there never e'er has been.
Anything more captivating than a tranquil wintry scene

All seasons blend together in perfect harmony
Each one's own uniqueness ... an orchestral symphony
Nature is beguiling ... so pleasing to the eye
Each season so varied and alluring ... love them all 'til I die

TURBULENCE AND PEACE

At times, our lives are turbulent and noisy
Yet other days are peaceful and great
Mother Nature likens it to a river
As it flows from state to state

Shallow streams run very swiftly
Negotiating underlying rocks and plants
As these obstacles cause barbarous currents
Water maddens like a gang of angry ants

Deep counterparts run smooth and gracefully
Despite the impediments below
They glide along quite effortlessly
With a calm and gentle flow
Compare a river to our lives because when our lives are full
Every hour of the day seems great... things are never dull

So the next time you're a little downhearted
And feeling out of your class
Cheer up and laugh it off
For, without a doubt ... it'll pass!

PLAGIARISM

Plagiarism in its entirety is to steal another man's work
And to use it as his own
A simple poem or a work of art
That's been worked on from dusk 'til dawn
Plagiarism of this form is despicable
Without a doubt it's deceitful and wrong
But surely in other contexts
Ideas can be borrowed from a song
After all ... every thing we know
We have gained from generations past
Teachers, professors so full of learning
With an abundance of knowledge e'er so vast
We're taught from the day we're born
In kindergarten and the junior school class
We're taught how to copy the masters
The gifted ... and those with exuberant brash
Plays and films have been copied
From Shakespeare, Lewis Carol and more
But film makers and playwrights
Put a different slant on their score

Scrooge, a favourite character
Especially during Christmas and festive time
Has been written by many a dramatist
Adding his own ideas, themes or rhyme

So, plagiarism can be justified
As long as ideas are not used word for word
The conception must come from within oneself
Like brilliance ... in the song of a bird.
Yes, every type of wildlife mimic each other
It's a very special thing they do
And just like all animals in the forest
We humans are blameworthy too

So go about your creation
Write down what really comes through
A basic idea may be borrowed
But your main inner thoughts must ring true

AN EARLY MORNING CLIMB OVER PENDLE HILL

I set off early one morning, in the blossoming dawn
O'er a vast grassy lea ... a deep evergreen lawn
More beautiful sights I ne'er have seen
A more beautiful morning there ne'er has been
Over hanging sallows fluttering in caliginous light
Elm leaves forming a pattern e'er so bright
Swaying in the breeze ... tender ears of corn
Abiding by nature's laws ... as a new life reborn

The call of a night bird ... a most beautiful sound
Movement of grass wavering on the ground
A most calming feeling that only quietness heaves
And silence broken by rustling leaves
Treading o'er a moor ... a vast open lea
A vast ocean of land ... a green open sea
Approaching the foot of the great hill ... e'er so steep
Home to rabbits, deer and flocks of sheep

Young Spring lambs feeding from mother hew
Playing and intermingling in the early morning dew
An arduous uphill climb o'er a steep grassy incline
Encouraged onwards by scenic views e'er so divine

Browsing as I stood on top of Pendle Hill
A cool air so refreshing ... so very still
From the east I was greeted by the early morning sun
A sign that a new day had just begun
Dazzling rays lit up the sky e'er so bright
Birds from their nest took to the air in flight
An abundance of wild flowers and tall green shoots
Species of organic plants with bulbous roots

Various small shrubs and wild briar intertwined
A diverse ecosystem to soothe the mind
To the north, a cluster of hamlets and winding vales
And beyond ... the gateway to the Yorkshire Dales
The Forest of Bowland ... a sight to behold
Surrounded by vistas of a beauty untold
Mesmerised by it all ... 'twas a moment sublime
Enthralled by nature's beauty ... unaltered by time

Standing in open air on top of the world
'Neath snowy white clouds all bulbous and curled
A deep inner feeling enveloped me like ne'er has been
A feeling of contentment ... so clear, so clean
To amble o'er Pendle Hill unlocks a secret ... enabling a soul to bask
Well worth the effort of a pleasant, yet difficult task!

This poem is to enlighten the fact that little thing we do in life make a big difference

SMALL DEEDS

A Tiny boy played on a beach
The day after a torrential gale
When he noticed thousands of starfish
Stranded way inland, looking delicately frail

The poor wretched creatures struggled onwards
With tentacles all tattered and torn
Instinct driving them relentlessly seawards
Back to the ocean from whence they were born

Stranded way back from the water
Struggling to crawl through sun beaten sand
The little boy's heart felt all woozy
And he decided to give them a hand

He realised the starfish's plight was imminent
And that he'd to act as fast as could be
So he picked up one of the tiny creatures
And then trudged a mile to the sea

Much later, returning to the scene
He picked up another dying fish
When a man approached and asked him
"What are you doing lad... what is your wish?"

"I'm goin' to chuck all these poor things back,"
Said the youngster with a serious face
Then without any further ado
He headed seaward increasing his pace

"Hold on there young fella!"
Said the bloke with a kind of deep reverence
"I think you're acting rather kind
But, believe me, it won't make any difference"

But then ... from the mouth of a babe
Came an innocent reply, hitting the man like a bomb
"Oh I think you're wrong there mister
I'll make 'eck of a difference to this one!"

A COUNTRYSIDE WALK

A countryside stroll is relaxing
To breathe in and smell pure fresh air
To hear the sound of forest creatures
So soothing, refreshing and fair
Whether it be autumn, winter or summer
Or the first whisper of spring
There's nothing on earth so refreshing
Than to espy a bird on the wing

Cows happily chewing their cud
Young lambs playing in leas
Rabbits scurrying to their burrows
Magial events set the body at ease
A sensation encompasses one's being
Making nerve ends tingle and thrive
The mind becomes calmed and settled
And the entire body feels vibrantly alive

DAWN OF A. NEW DAY

Opening my eyes one summer morning
The sun shone way up high
Rays of silver shimmering light
Lit up a clear blue sky

Birds fluttering 'tween leafy trees
In a natural synchronized throng
Celebrating a brand new day
With a sweet melodious song

A rooster crowed in the distance.
Standing proudly at the helm
Flaunting its tail feathers proudly
Drawing attention to his realm

Countryside adorned in dazzling colours
Each with its own distinguished hue
Meadowlands revealing their secrets
'Tween the early morning dew

To me the event is magical
And it fills my heart with joy
Filtrating my nerve ends with gladness
It's been like that since I was a boy

Dawn is a beholding gift
A precious gift to all mankind
Take it, breathe it, embrace it
'Tis a path to peace of mind

DUSK IN THE COUNTRYSIDE

Dusk approaches on a bright summer's evening
Billowing red clouds float about way up high
Unbelievable beauty tends to unfold
And a magical painting envelops the sky

The sun begins to lower and set
Shimmering quicksilver embraces a full moon
Stars flicker 'gainst a dark laden sky
As if dancing to a heavenly tune

Darkness descends like a welcoming blanket
Encouraging nature to slow down and rest
Forest creatures migrate to their burrows
Birds settle down in their nests

Woodland silence is soothing and golden
It has a special sound of its own
Only broken by nocturnal creatures
Which forage woods from dusk till dawn

A COUNTRY STROLL

Nothing is more beautiful or expressing
The silhouette of a stunning blue lake
Mother Nature enhances its glamour
Mountain forests mirrored in its wake

Strolling alongside the banks of a country river
White water rapids crashing 'gainst rocky stones
Star-back fish darting hither and thither
Gathering insects from mossy inlet zones

Towering trees gaze down from the heavens
Making one feel so humble and small
My mind travels back... I am seven
Just a boy ... and boy, I'm having a ball

The majestic trees ... standing e'er so proud
Smile at me with an amiable greeting
My imagination triggers ... they're whispering out loud
"We've enjoyed this memorable meeting"

Nothing more beautiful than a tree ... that's true
Especially, leaves dripping with early morning dew
Sun shining through its branches with a glistening effect
No artist could e'er capture ... a scene e'er so perfect

A magical moment if one happens on the scene
So bewitching ... so stunning ... e'er so serene
Nothing in the world could ever more graceful be
Standing proudly alone in all its majesty

Birds foraging during wintry months
For worms, mites or any other type of food
Braving cruel winds and other feral elements
Striving to nourish their tiny brood

I gaze around and what do I see?
A peregrine swooping down on its prey
I hear little fledglings twittering in a tree
Parent birds ardently foraging day by day

Woodland creatures under a clear blue sky
Enjoying all the noise they can make
Nestling chicks learnin' to fly
Ducklings venturing onto an icy lake

Strolling carefree along ... I love to feel
Fresh spring winds blowing gently on my face
To smell the sweet fragrance of many flowers
Blooming hither and thither ... all o'er the place
Inhaling deep breathes

Cleansing fresh air of the fall
To the depths of one's inner self
Purifying body, mind and soul

The pure countryside air is amiable and free
Yet unaccountable ... is its worth
Take it, grab it ... any chance you can
Nothing is more precious ... upon this Earth

I was born just prior to the Second World War. Times were hard but people pulled together in adversary and helped each other through struggle and strife.

WAR YEARS

War was on the horizon on the day I was born
Hitler was causing havoc throughout town and city
People wer' feeling downcast, depressed and forlorn
British spirit kicked in and souls became very witty

An answer not to yield was to collect iron and steel
Thus folk arranged a scrap drive in order to survive
'Twas an emotional appeal ... enthusiasm was real
Causing Hitler to retreat and take a nose dive

To raise morale was the most important thing
Jokes wer' printed in papers and on billboards
Hopes wer' raised and people began to sing
Laughter could be heard throughout hills and fords

Blackout was the order of the day
Not a chink of light could be seen
'Twas a way of keeping German bombers at bay
And the night wardens became very keen

During the blackout it wer' hard for local folks
Mostly if flags were wet and slippy
But nobody bothered and they used to make jokes
Especially making their way to't chippy
Another thing that people didn't like
Was when rationing came to the fore
But folk took a hike or rode a bike
And swapped commodities fro' door to door

Black market was rife and caused people to cheat
But they didn't always do it in a hurry
But now and again they'd have a little treat
Especially fro' back of a lorry

Wartime was not a nice thing
But at least it brought people together
However, at its end the entire nation began to sing
T'was good for folks at th'end of their tether

A FLOWER

A flower's fragrance is so pure and sweet
Its perfume is an alluring essence
Blooming in a garden for me is a great treat
I feel uplifted whenever in their presence

Pansies always appear delicate and fragile
Yet they survive wind, hail and snow
During winter with heads held high they smile
And put on a glistening operatic show

Tulips and daffodils in their ephemeral state
Have their own unique fantastic flare
In springtime a rare beauty is their blessed fate
To dance like fairies blowing in the air

Beautiful roses with thorns e'er so sharp
Blowing gracefully in the wind so smooth and lush
With fragrance exquisite like a musical harp
Nothing more tranquil than a briar rose bush

Even wild flowers put on a fantastic show
As they are pollinated by bumble bees
Food for tiny insects as they come and go
Complimented by birds singing in verdant trees

Daisies, buttercups and dandelions are special too
As they browse and dance in fields of grass
Each one displays its own unique hue
And elegantly displays colours of vibrant class

A synopsis of my life just to let you know where I'm coming from.

MY LIFE

Turn around I was two
Turn around I was four
Turn around, turn around
I was a young boy going out of the door

In infant class I made a lot o' noise
Chasing girls and playing with toys
It wer' a catholic school and run by a nun
But she never e'er stopped me having loads o' fun

At seven I went into junior school
All the kids wer' poor but e'er so cool
Lads wore steel bottom clogs that made a great sound
Creating bright sparks by kicking the ground

At eleven I attended Towneley Tech, a school in a park
I got into mischief ... anything for a lark
I was unhappy and didn't study for a long spell
When the exams came along I didn't fair very well

So at fifteen ... down a coalmine I had to go
Came home every night black as black fro' head to toe
But I enjoyed it and ... workin' as hard as one can
I grew big and strong ... it made me a man

Five years I worked down that dark dank hole
But I earned good money ... better than being on't dole
At twenty the pit closed and into the army I went
For the next two years ... time as a soldier I spent

National service called me up to serve in the medical core
'Twas then that my nursing skills came to the fore
Nursing in African field hospitals I worked hand in hand
Alongside trained soldiers ... the pick of the land

Two years later I was back in Civvy Street
T'was then my first wife I happened to meet
I was as fit as a fiddle but I didn't have a dime
No option but to spend more years down a mine

At twenty-seven I then became a proud dad
My wife gave birth to a bonny wee lad
I quit working the mine near to a coal delph
And decided to start working for myself

I did well and drove all around the British Isles
Lots of money ... lots of smiles
I was working in Clydebank ... I became e'er so glad
Wife had given birth to another wee lad

At thirty-eight I changed course without any fear
And decided to make nursing my future career
I finished up working in Casualty ... 'twas my fate
Deeds came to me naturally ... a special trait

My wife and I parted ... what could I do
During my off time I met bride number two
She was a blonde and bubbly with beautiful eyes
Every time she passed me I felt queer in mi' thighs

Sadly, she became ill and God called her to go
We'd spent fifteen years together ... I loved her so
At sixty I couldn't go on and for what it's worth
I decided to up sticks and travel the earth

To enjoy life and exploit it ... I made it my aim
I went to Greece, America and many countries you can name
Down the Colorado River rapids I rafted 'neath a burning sun
'Twas as though my life had just begun

Then for years I traversed through sunshine and thunderous rain
On a pilgrimage o'er mountains in northern Spain
The mountain people were friendly, generous and clannish
'Twas there that I picked up the language of Spanish

Finally I went to Australia and met the love of my life
Two years later she became my third wife
For a while we lived in Tasmania 'mongst hills and dales
Now we're back in Burnley with all its rain and gales

We've been married seven years now
And passed the seven year itch
I'm blessed and happy
And for sure ... I **feel rich**

I've got a creaky back an' mi knees are on the wane
But there's no way I'm goin' to fret
'Cos ... in spite of all the aches and pains
There's plenty o' life in the old dog yet

The last three poems are about wild animals living in theirnatural habit. Animals definitely live by the laws of nature and God's laws and thus, I class them as biblical

WILDEBEASTS

The dry season in the Serengeti is dramatic
Creating the greatest wildlife spectacle on earth,
More than two million wilderbeast, zebra and gazelles
Cross over the River Mara for all their worth.

As wilderbeasts slide down a slippery bank
Crocodiles sidle underwater awaiting their prey
Herds fighting 'gainst torrential under currents
And anything else that comes their way.

Many animals drown in the rip roaring water
Hundreds more are eaten alive,
But because of the countless numbers
Thousands crash on relentlessly and survive.

Crossing the Mara River is a very menacing task
But more danger ahead is their blessed fate,
They have now entered into a lion's kingdom
Where predators hide in bush country and wait.

'Tis an opportune time for hungry lions
Who know a steady food supply is at bay,
Lionesses organise themselves in groups
Each one ideally positioned alongside the way.

Herds are now in the Masal Mara Region
A large area of open grasslands,
Where they can rest and cautiously graze
And fullfil all their bodily demands.

'Tis a pageant carried out year after year
'Tis the only way wild animals survive,
But despite all the ordeals and setbacks
Wildlife creatures endure, up and thrive.

What compels the magnificent animals onwards
'Tis not yet completely understood,
But this magnificent spectacle goes on forever
Under tempests, lightning and flood.

LIONS

The Serengeti is in East Africa
Spanning parts of the Tanzanian Plain,
Open rolling grasslands and scattered acacia thickets
Parched and bare due to lack of rain.

'Tis a hostile environment for many wild animals
Who strive to survive year after year,
Foraging in dense riverine swamps and jungles
For young ones they have to rear.

Lions are so different with a technique of their own
And they form a coalition known as a pride,
And when on the hunt for their prey
They are astute and attack side by side.

After a long dark night in the jungle
Dawn comes around fast on the run,
A carpet of dark velvet is replaced by
Dazzling rays of a new morning sun

The air shudders to the sound of a lion
A roar that can be heard miles away,
A male contacts members of his pride
Also a warning to keep other creatures at bay.

When a male cub reaches the age of two
From the pride he is forced to depart.
It then becomes known as a nomad
And a self hunting he has to start

It joins up with other nomads
And together they set up a scheme,
Together they become mightily forceful
And create a most formidable team.

On reaching the age of five
A male lion is in his prime,
He's powerful, dominant and majestic
And has reached a magical time.

'Tis time to assert his authority
And to challenge longstanding prides,
To take over from elderly males
And take the lionesses as his brides.

To assure his pride is successful
An alliance has to be made firm and strong,
Placing him at the head of the pride
Enabling him to sire lots of young.

A male lion's reign as chief is relatively short
Due to its commensurate life span
But a lion is a resilient creature
And it'll be king for as long as it can.

There are many more creatures in the Seringeti
And each one displays its own unique flair,
But his majesty the lion with his shaggy mane
Is 'King of the jungle,' in his own quirky lair.

WILD ANIMALS

I've always been a wild animal fan
And read about 'em whenever I can
They live by nature's law all the time
Creating a natural rythym and rhyme

Unlike mankind who kills for gain
They hunt prey only so as to survive
It helps to keep the balance in main
And to feed and keep young one's alive

Scavengers play an important roll
Vultures strip a carcass with ease
Hyenas too are on the ball
Keeping at bay any risk of disease

Elephants tread o'er long standing tracks
Depositing dung and fruit bearing seeds
Soaked up in dry land cracks
To blossom into tree bearing feeds

Animals ask for no more than to survive
To care for their family and young
Even insects and snakes play their part
Dung beetles thrive on elephant dung

Hippos are of a different class
And oft' tend to go off the rails
They trudge along through tall river grass
Creating long life giving river trails

A wildlife mother's instinct is rife
To rear her young is an effectuate agenda
She'll protect them at the cost of her life
With courage, love and awesome splendour

Mankind should work alongside wildlife
Even take a tip from their life style
And maybe relieve some human strife
And pick up a hint of nature's guile

Just to finish off my book I enclose a few quotes from The Book Of Wisdom & Proverbs. I sincerely hope they guide you and help to keep you on the right path.

Your life is but a mist, it will appear for just a while and disappear in a cloud

A wise man builds his house on rock A house built on sand will surely fall

From the abundance of the heart the mouth speaks

The heavens declare the glory of God, the firmament encapsulates and declares his handiwork

There is no speech or language that is not heard

The lamp of integrity glows brightly ... the lamp of the wicked fades

Wisdom is a fountain of life ... it avoids the snares of death

Withstanding trials of faith begets patience

Patience begets purity and integrity

As the sun parches grass and flowers, so will a rich man wither away

No man or soul is tempted by God

A soul is tempted by his own passion

The tongue is a fire ... the very world of iniquity

Every type of beast can be tamed by mankind. Yet the tongue ... no man can tame

A wise man shows good deeds in the meekness of wisdom

Wisdom is peaceful, docile, moderate and chaste

Daffodils neither toil nor spin, yet Solomon in all his glory did not compare

Be a soul of integrity and no torment shall touch thee

An evil man is full of guile and deceit

The throat is an open sepulchre so guard thy tongue
Our lifetime is but a fleeting moment, it will be pursued by the sun and evaporate

Live thy life with purity, virtue and integrity

Put away from thee false speech. Truthful lips endure forever, the lying tongue for only a moment

Bind kindness and fidelity around thy neck

Happy be the man who begets wisdom and integrity

A man of integrity may rest and his sleep is full of peace

A wise man does not choose the way of a lawless man

A wise man inherits honour, a foolish man inherits shame

Embrace wisdom and she shall exalt thee

To be wise is to thy own advantage,

The mouth of the just yields wisdom and peace
The mouth of the wicked yields perversion

He who guards his tongue is wise

A rich man can have nothing whereas a poor man can be very rich

Better a poor man of integrity than a rich wicked man

A wicked man steps into a snare, a just man walks joyfully

To advance in grace, forsake foolishness and seek wisdom

Before all things, wisdom was created

Avoid wickedness and it will turn aside from thee

Do no evil and evil will not overtake thee

Delight not in telling a lie, for it never results in good

More and more humble thy pride for what awaits man is worms

Before man are life and death, whichever he chooses shall be given to him

Like dew that abates a burning wind, so does a kind word improve a gift

Wisdom keeps a man good in all aspects; when sin is rife he avoids wrong doing

Rely not on deceitful wealth for it will not help on the day of wrath

Be constant in your thoughts, steadfast in your words

How irksome wisdom is to the unruly! The fool cannot abide her

Put thy feet into the fettles of wisdom and thy neck under her yoke

Bear wisdom as your role of glory, bear her as your crown

If thou sees a man of prudence; let thy feet wear away his doorstep

A man of integrity and virtue keeps his way straight

He who has eyes/ears... let him see/hear

The sands of the seashore, the drops of rain, the days of eternity: who can number these?

Heaven's height, earth's breadth, the depth of the abyss: who can explore them?

Sow not the furrows of the injustice, lest thou harvest it sevenfold

Avoid wickedness and it will flee from thee

The flute and the harp offer sweet melody, but better than both is a voice that is true

Blessed indeed is the majestic beauty of a rainbow

Wisdom is a stream whose runlets gladden the heavens

A person of integrity sets forth riddles to the music of a harp

Never let the tongue give free speech to evil talk

Act good against evil and God will tip the scales in your favour

God will meet your needs but not always your wants
Integrity glows like stars in the sky

Be consistent in your thoughts and steadfast in thy words

A man's conscience tells him more than seven men of high esteem

Made in the USA
Columbia, SC
02 October 2024